A Starchamber Quiry

A James Joyce Centennial Volume
1882–1982

A Starchamber Quiry

A James Joyce Centennial Volume 1882–1982

HUGH KENNER

FRITZ SENN

E.L. EPSTEIN

ROBERT BOYLE, SJ

With an Afterword by
CLIVE HART

Edited by
E.L. EPSTEIN

METHUEN

NEW YORK AND LONDON

For William York Tindall

First published in 1982 by
Methuen & Co. Ltd
11 New Fetter Lane, London EC4P 4EE

Published in the USA by
Methuen & Co.
in association with Methuen, Inc.
733 Third Avenue, New York,
NY 10017

Printed in Great Britain at the
University Press, Cambridge

British Library Cataloguing in Publication Data

A starchamber quiry: a James Joyce centennial
volume, 1882–1982.
I. Kenner, Hugh   II. Epstein, E.L.
823'.912[F]   PR6019.09Z/

ISBN 0-416-31560-7

Library of Congress Cataloging in Publication Data
Main entry under title:

A Starchamber quiry.

  1. Joyce, James, 1882–1941—Criticism and interpretation
—Addresses, essays, lectures.   I. Kenner,
Hugh.   II. Epstein, Edmund L.
PR 6019.09Z8125   1982   823'.912   81-16929

ISBN 0-416-31560-7   AACR2

Contents

Acknowledgements   vi
Abbreviations   vii
Introduction   ix

James Joyce and his civilization   1
   Hugh Kenner, Notes toward an anatomy of
   'modernism'   3

James Joyce and his orders   43
   Fritz Senn, Weaving, unweaving   45

James Joyce and the body   71
   E. L. Epstein, James Joyce and the body 73

James Joyce and the soul   107
   Robert Boyle, SJ, Worshipper of the Word: James
   Joyce and the Trinity   109

James Joyce and his readers   153
   Clive Hart, Afterword: reading *Finnegans Wake* 155

Acknowledgements

The editor and publisher would like to thank the following for permission to reproduce copyright material: The Bodley Head and Random House, Inc., for extracts from *Ulysses*; The Society of Authors and Viking Penguin, Inc., for extracts from *Finnegans Wake* (© 1939 by James Joyce, renewed 1967 by George and Lucia Joyce); Princeton University Press for extracts from Dante Alighieri, *The Divine Comedy*, trans. Charles Singleton, 1970.

Abbreviations

P   *A Portrait of the Artist as a Young Man*, ed. Chester G. Anderson (New York, Viking Press, 1964)

U   *Ulysses* (New York, Random House, 1961) (the reset edition)

FW *Finnegans Wake* (New York, Viking Press, 1939; London, Faber, 1939)

Letters, I, II and III *Letters of James Joyce*, vol. I, ed. Stuart Gilbert (New York, Viking Press, 1957); vols II and III, ed. Richard Ellmann (New York, Viking Press, 1966)

Those four claymen clomb together to hold their sworn starchamber quiry on him. For he was ever their quarrel, the way they would see themselves. (*FW* 475. 18–20)

How sweet the moonlight sleeps upon this bank!
Here will we sit and let the sounds of music
Creep in our ears; soft stillness and the night
Become the touches of sweet harmony.
Sit, Jessica. Look how the floor of heaven
Is thick inlaid with patens of bright gold.
There's not the smallest orb which thou behold'st
But in his motion like an angel sings
Still quiring to the young-ey'd cherubins.
(Shakespeare, *The Merchant of Venice*, V. i. 54–62)

Introduction

Joyce planned to follow [*Our Exagmination*], which he designated by
the symbol O, by X, a book of four long essays (for the *Wake*'s four old
men) on the subjects of the treatment of night, mechanics and
chemistry, humor, and one other which on May 28 [1929] he had not
yet determined.   (Richard Ellmann, *James Joyce*
      (London and New York, Oxford University Press, 1959), p. 626)

James Joyce was, like Leopold Bloom, interested professionally in
advertisement and promotion. He encouraged his friends to
produce a volume of explication for *Finnegans Wake* and he
wished to follow it up by another volume, which he designated as
X. This volume was to consist of four long essays on various
aspects of the *Wake*. The four old men in the *Wake* represent all
attempts at the ordering of experience – the four cardinal
directions, the four gospels, the Four Masters (Irish historians)
and so on; accompanied by their donkey they trail through the
Wake as comic figures attempting to understand the nature of the
huge hero of the *Wake*, and his family. The quadripartite
commentary on the *Wake* never appeared. Perhaps this book is
finally Joyce's X.

This volume, designed to celebrate the centenary of Joyce's
birth (2 February 1882), is different in some ways from Joyce's X.
There are five contributors, not four; Joyce seems to have
forgotten that the four old men's donkey is formidably articulate,
so the present volume is more Joycean than its model. Also, it is
not exclusively on the *Wake*. In addition, the original X was
supposed to contain four rather miscellaneous essays, while this
volume contains five pieces that are organized to treat most
aspects of Joyce's work. However, the miscellaneous nature of
Joyce scholarship is fully represented in this volume. Two pieces
– the essays by Hart and Kenner – are in a humanistic tradition;
they are commentaries on Joyce's times and warnings about

critical excess by writers on Joyce. The remaining essays are in a more analytical mode – Senn, Epstein and Boyle engage in close analysis of the texts of *Ulysses* and *Finnegans Wake*. It is for the reader to decide whether these three essays are of the type warned against by Hart. So the critics of Joyce meet, and collide, and meet again, which is as it should be. The four old men and their donkey in *Finnegans Wake* do not succeed in describing the hero adequately either. When a time comes he reveals himself.

Any writer has five aspects: a participation in history, a style, a body, a soul and a memory to his readers. It is these five aspects which order this volume. Hugh Kenner, in 'Notes toward an anatomy of "modernism"', describes the civilization that produced Joyce and influenced his outlook on the world: a world organized into modern cities, machine-ordered and filled with modern crowds. The rhythms of the machine fill the pages of Joyce; the rhythms of the typewriter and the needs of a modern society shape the composition of Joyce's texts. Fritz Senn, in 'Weaving, unweaving', describes a characteristic of Joyce's style, the deliberate disruption of patterns; The Principle of the Disrupted Pattern, as Senn describes it, represents the final stage of a reader's appreciation of Joycean style. At first the text often seems a pure and simple jangle of words; then, as the reader becomes more expert in reading Joyce, the patterns begin to emerge. At this point, the reader is tempted to consider the works of Joyce as over-organized, over-determined to the last dot and dash. However, Senn's analysis of Joyce comes to the reader's assistance, with the description of Joyce's style as characterized certainly by patterning, but by a disrupted patterning. E. L. Epstein's essay 'James Joyce and the body' describes how the body operating on the soul produces the creative works of the artist and the mature man. Father Boyle's essay, 'Worshipper of the Word: James Joyce and the Trinity', takes the analysis one step further, to a description of the soul of the human being and the nature of the Trinity and its equivalent in the human soul. Finally, Clive Hart, in his breathtakingly sensible 'Afterword: reading *Finnegans Wake*', provides an account of the experience of one reader with the text of the *Wake* and a guide for other readers. Hart and Senn together provide an antidote to the over-systematization that is an ever-present temptation for Joyceans. However, none of the three analytical essays purports to be anything more than a partial explication of some aspects of Joyce's work. Like the realities he claimed to represent, Joyce's works always exhaust the enquiring mind. 'The squirming facts exceed the squamous mind,' as Wallace Stevens writes, 'if one may say so.'

James Joyce was, in a real sense, both his body *and* his works. Joyce seems to have believed sincerely in the scholastic division of entities into 'substance' and 'accidents'. The combined 'substance' of James Augustine Aloysius Joyce − his soul and body − made its bow to the world on 2 February 1882. However, the substance began to acquire different 'accidents' shortly after his birth − a civilization, a memory, an education, a set of experiences, a language, several languages. His substance began to flow on to paper in Joyce's early years with the publication of 'Et Tu, Healy', and increasingly came to be composed of paper and ink. On 13 January 1941, the substance of Joyce lost its fleshy envelope and became entirely words on paper and in the minds of his readers.

Joyce describes this process in *Finnegans Wake*. Shem the Penman writes all over his own body with his own 'wastes' until he has transformed his 'accidents' into literature: 'reflecting from his own individual person life unlivable, transaccidentated through the slow fires of consciousness into a dividual chaos' (*FW* 186.3−5). In this sense the substance of Joyce is still with us, 'transaccidentated' into millions of copies of his works. Therefore, on 2 February 1982, the substance of Joyce will be a hundred years old. 'The word that would not pass away' (*FW* 186.6) has achieved its first century mark.

E. L. Epstein

James Joyce
and
his civilization

Notes toward an anatomy of 'modernism'

HUGH KENNER

Modernism, la la. Yet it once had brave days.

> An American called Eliot called this P.M. . . . . He has actually
> trained himself *and* modernized himself *on his own*. . . . It is
> such a comfort to meet a man and not have to tell him to wash
> his face, wipe his feet, and remember the date (1914) on the
> calendar.[1]

Ezra Pound to Harriet Monroe; and note the prescriptive force of
the verb 'modernized'. Formerly 'modern' had meant little more
than 'in the manner of today'; thus you might modernize a text by
eliminating old spellings, or you might study a modern language,
the French they speak now instead of the Latin they spoke
formerly. Also by contagion with *à la mode* – merely 'in fashion' –
'modern' could carry pejorative overtones; Swift complained
(1757) of scribblers who corrupted English by 'abominable
curtailings and quaint modernisms', and the *OED* cites the
coupling 'imperfections and modernisms' from a source as late as
1897.

Somehow, in Pound's usage, 'modernize' has become a moral
imperative, in a drastic way that comports with our intuition of a
new age beginning rather suddenly.

It was in his apprehension of *what* had changed that James Joyce
differed from the fellow modernists of his generation. For as we
may glean from *Finnegans Wake*, a ringing of changes on 'the same
anew' was his summary view of the human adventure in history.

Vico's Three Ages came to afford him a model for what does after all alter, but these Ages are as alike as they are different, and do not make headway but recycle. Talk of 'modern man' enjoying the advantages of no longer being mired in the nineteenth century did not spring as readily to Joyce's lips as, for instance, to Pound's; Joyce felt constrained to 'remember the date on the calendar' only for the sake of getting minutiae of detail and costume right. *Writing* changed for Joyce: that is spectacularly true: all the way from the 'scrupulous meanness' of *Dubliners* to Wakese, and in just a couple of decades. But to locate him amid the other modernists we must understand how thoroughly they are characterized by a conviction he seems not to have shared: that early in the century something *external to writing* had changed, and in changing obligated a change in artistic means. And the most striking thing about this alteration on which so many agreed is the consensus about its suddenness.

Virginia Woolf was whimsically willing to supply an exact date. It was 'on or about December 1910', she wrote, that 'human character changed',[2] forcing literature to absorb a massive change that had taken place outside itself: to forgo its millennial habit of evolving from within.

What had changed? Though the portents of 1910 included the return of Halley's comet, cosmic explanations may not wholly satisfy, Halley's comet having effected nothing noticeable at its previous appearance in 1833. And 'human character'? There is no way we can locate in retrospect a change in human character.

Human character, though, may be shaped by the conditions amid which human lives are conducted. A sufficiently comprehensive change in those conditions, amounting to a change in the quality of life, is something we might hope to recognize. And, yes, there had been such a change, a concurrence of particular changes, rapid enough to have been readily perceived by people coming to maturity in 1910: the year in which Pound was 25, and Eliot 22, and James Joyce 28. (The daemonic Picasso, for that matter, was 29, and William Butler Yeats an unserene 45.)

What was it all of them saw? Observe to begin with that they were all urban men. Pound had grown up near Philadelphia, Eliot in St Louis and Cambridge (Mass.), Joyce in the Dublin he called 'the seventh city of Christendom' (*P* 167). (And Picasso, Barcelona/Paris; and Yeats, Dublin/London.) What had suddenly altered, within the young manhood of that generation, was the quality of city life. It had altered thanks to what a historian of vorticist painting has accurately called 'The First Machine Age'.[3]

Though better publicized, the industrial revolution of a century previously had been a comparatively remote affair, rather easy to ignore if you stayed away from the places it engulfed. It installed dark satanic mills in Leeds and Bradford but changed London very little. The lanes of London as late as the 1880s were still scavenged by municipal goats, one of which chased an acquaintance of the painter Whistler to the door of his club. A street on which you may encounter a goat is not yet a street in an industrial city.

But by 1900 the Machine was all around, and the most evident thing it facilitated was the Crowd. The London Underground was being electrified, and in Dublin (of all places) they were acquiring the most up-to-date electric tram system in Europe. These systems were sired by that symbol that so overwhelmed Henry Adams, the dynamo; Joyce records something new in the urban sound-scape, 'the whirr of flapping leathern bands and hum of dynamos from the powerhouse' (U 242). The horsedrawn tram on whose platform adolescent Stephen bade a girl idyllic farewell ('No sound broke the peace of the night save when the lank brown horses rubbed their noses together and shook their bells' (P 69)) is a pastoral memory by 1904: 'Right and left parallel clanging ringing a doubledecker and a singledeck moved from their railheads, swerved to the down line, glided parallel' (U 116). And apprentices no longer lived above their shops; in the world's metropolises hordes of wage-earners were being shipped in each morning and out again each evening, and were also turned loose on the streets at lunchtime. City streets had never before supported such crowds: 'trampled by insistent feet', wrote Eliot, 'At four and five and six o'clock' (Preludes, IV. 3–4). Nor did Eliot, newly come to London from America, fail to notice that unlike Americans Londoners in a crowd keep their eyes lowered: 'And each man fixed his eyes before his feet' (The Waste Land, I. 65).

Each morning, cued by urban mass-transport schedules, many thousand alarm clocks rang:

> One thinks of all the hands
> That are raising dingy shades
> In a thousand furnished rooms.   (Preludes, II. 8–10)

It had been a commonplace of former literature that human lives were governed by the seasons, spring, summer, autumn, winter. Now they were being governed by the *time*, ascertained to the nearest five minutes. Joyce's friend Frank Budgen, another lifelong city man, put this concisely:

> James Watt invented the steam engine, and the steam engine begat the locomotive, and the locomotive begat the timetable, forcing people to . . .think in minutes where their great-grandfathers thought in hours. . . . The discoveries of the astronomer and the mathematician have less immediate effect on [social time-sense] than the electrification of the suburban lines.[4]

That crowds were a new phenomenon was something the futurist painters were early to note. Crowds filled streets not only to celebrate coronations and military victories but daily, except Sunday, at eight, at noon, and at five, to celebrate nothing. Ugo Boccioni and Wyndham Lewis both painted dense abstract pictures called *The Crowd*, and Lewis entitled a piece of vorticist prose 'The Crowd-Master'. A crowd-man's experience of life was governed by discontinuities and cued by omnipresent machines.

> when the human engine waits
> Like a taxi throbbing waiting
> *(The Waste Land*, III. 216–17)

wrote Eliot, who also noted the effect of the internal combustion engine on the contemporary perception of rhythm. In

> Who pays the rent?
> Yes he pays the rent
> Well some men don't and some men do
> Some men don't and you know who
> *(Sweeney Agonistes*, I. 5–8)

we can hear an idling four-cylinder with an unreliable spark. Eliot also hinted at an undissociated sensibility which should form new wholes out of the sound of the typewriter and the smell of cooking. Jacob Epstein's *Rock Drill* (1912) incorporated an actual pneumatic drill, ruthless in its functional contours and identical in sculptural idiom with the helmet-headed machine-man who crouched around and above it, engaged in what Lewis in another connection called 'its disastrous polished dance'.[5] *Rock Drill* epitomized a new interpenetration of machines and normal experience; the motor car was requiring paved, not cobbled, roads, and the need to break into pavement when a city's arteries required surgery was bringing the pavement drill into the city, and its clamor to beneath a poet's windows.

Above its din a poet at a typewriter (making a poem out of mechanical letters) might hear a telephone jingle. Its bell was a rhythmic novelty –

> Ting a ling ling
> Ting a ling ling

– in Eliot's jazzed transcription, but what happened when you picked up the receiver –

> Pick up the receiver
> What'll I say?   (*Sweeney Agonistes*, I. 31–2; 40–1)

– was novelty of another order entirely, particularly when, a decade into the century, the telephone was ceasing to be a business machine and commencing to invade the home and the furnished flat. For though its wires are strung like telegraph wires, the telephone accosts us with a new order of experience. The telegram is but an expedited post, but the telephone brings a phantom presence into your ear: a recognizable but disembodied voice, its owner simultaneously *there* and *here*. 'Hello Hello are you there?' (*Sweeney Agonistes*, I. 45) is what Eliot's Dusty says when she does pick up the receiver; it is the pertinent question, and in England as late as the 1950s they were still saying something similar. For voice no longer signifies presence, and *The Waste Land* (1922 – just before *Sweeney Agonistes* gave metrical lines to a telephone bell) is an orchestration of disembodied voices. What still has power to disorient us in this poem is our inability to imagine any situation within which the speakers are present. This fact at one time bothered Eliot himself, and he thought of affixing 'Gerontion' as a preface, thus turning the voices of *The Waste Land* into

> Tenants of the house,
> Thoughts of a dry brain in a dry season.
>
> ('Gerontion', 75–6)

But Pound dissuaded him, and the poem retains its radical unlikeness to a Browning monologue. Historians may some day think it pertinent that Browning had never used a telephone. The ventriloquist was his model, or Mr Sludge the Medium, or the proprietor of a showman's booth.

Crowds, voices without bodies, artificial light, sad clock-bound shuttling, the omnipresent sound of machines defying nature: these urban sensations were never wholly alien to the English literary sensibility, shaped as that sensibility had been by *Paradise Lost*, the poem which 'with godlike foresight' (in Peter Conrad's words) 'contains the literature and the art of the two centuries which follow its composition.'[6] The ancient tension between city and country had been decided by Milton, and decided against the city, of which the paradigm was the city his devils construct in Hell, having 'rifl'd the bowels of their mother Earth' (*Paradise Lost*, I. 687) for metals: one reason Blake's mills are 'satanic'. And after they build Pandemonium, behold,

>   From the arched roof
> Pendant by subtle Magic many a row
> Of Starry Lamps and blazing Cressets fed
> With *Naphtha* and *Asphaltus* yielded light
> As from a sky   (*Paradise Lost*, I. 726–30)

which is more like 1900 London than like anything Milton knew; and the place is athrong with sad devils beyond number, the prototypical crowd. So when in Eliot's 'Unreal City'

> A crowd flowed over London Bridge, so many,
> I had not thought death had undone so many
>   (*The Waste Land*, I. 62–3)

the infernal decor, and the quotation from Dante whom Milton too more than once quoted, comport with the vision and with a traditional eloquence.

So Eliot in his most aggressively modernist poem could feel himself sustained by a strong tradition. What is 'modern' about *The Waste Land* is discontinuity, the commuter's pervasive experience. Am I glimpsing a face I know? Where did I know it? What are we both doing here?

> There I saw one I knew, and stopped him, crying:
>   'Stetson!
> 'You who were with me in the ships at Mylae! . . .'
>   (I. 69–70)

From London to Mylae, that is a temporal and conceptual discontinuity, readily recognized; 'Jutland', in 1922, would have been unsurprising. More subtle, more unsettling, more difficult to specify, is the poetic discontinuity that pervades modernism, installed as it is in the very conception of the poetic line, something newly detached from the continuities of the speaking voice.

One way to isolate this effect is to concentrate on the line, or on the word, as something to be not only spoken and heard but looked at. If we return to our poet as he puts down the telephone and resumes his typing, we may note that he is getting on with a job Milton could not do, dictating, nor Browning, scribbling: a job one cannot do with a pen in one's hand or in the hand of one's amanuensis. He is arranging words on a page in a precisely spaced mechanical grid. That was something printers had routinely done to words that Pope or Tennyson wrote by hand, but the look of a printed page (though it interested Pope) cannot be thought of as forming an important part of Tennyson's intention. Poetry looks like poetry, that's sufficient; and the look, with its unjustified right margin, was an accident merely of the packaging of the poem for the buyer.

The look of a printed page, though, is essential to a poem like Pound's 'The Return':

> . . . Gods of the winged shoe!
> With them the silver hounds
> > sniffing the trace of air!
>
> Haie! Haie!
> > These were the swift to harry;
> These were keen-scented;
> These were the souls of blood.
>
> Slow on the leash,
> > pallid the leash-men!

This is meant to look like a Greek poem on the page; in particular, the first stanza, which I've not transcribed, looks enough like a stanza of Sappho's to alert guiding memories. And with its left and right placements it isolates portions of lines as though for two choirs of voices, or as though, more abstractly, to designate tacit systems of subordination. The 'line' is no longer the enactment of a metrical norm, but a unit of quick attention:

> With them the silver hounds
>   sniffing the trace of air

and

> With them the silver hounds sniffing the trace of air

are not identical at all, though composed of identical words.

When Yeats deflected $200 toward him, Ezra Pound immediately invested in essentials: two Gaudier carvings, and a typewriter. A poet without a typewriter, in the new era, was a sculptor without a chisel. Pound, Eliot, Williams, all of them typed their poems, composed, even, in typing. The handwritten drafts of the *Pisan Cantos* (1945) contain the typewriter symbols, like '/' and '@ ', neatly written in. Marianne Moore at one time in her life even taught typewriting, and her conception of a stanza, in élite type on an $8\frac{1}{2} \times 11$ sheet of paper, was apt to be a visual pattern, repeated.

> Toward the high-keyed intermittent squeak
>   of broken carriage-springs, made by
> the three similar, meek-
>   coated bird's-eye-
> freckled forms she comes; and when
> from the beak
>   of one, the still living
>   beetle has dropped
> out, she picks it up and puts
> it in again.

That is a stanza of 'Bird-Witted', and in it we may discern with especial clarity the modernist conception of the line. It is no longer a rhetorical unit to guide the voice, like Tennyson's line:

> The long brook falling thro' the clov'n ravine
> In cataract after cataract, to the sea

– since the end of the line no longer need cue a syntactic pause. No, the line has become *a typographical unit*. The reason 'the three similar, meek-' is a line in 'Bird-Witted' is that the pattern exacts a grouping of that length at that point in the stanza. And if the onomatopoeic 'squeak' is echoed by 'meek' and again by 'beak', all in line-end positions, that is an effect the line happens to isolate, though the reading voice had better not unless it is going to fragment the sense utterly. Another pair of rhymes, 'by' and 'eye', is equally isolated by the lineation but cannot be acknowledged by the voice at all, since at all costs the voice must follow the syntactic unit 'made by / the three similar, meek- / coated bird's-eye- / freckled forms', and syntax forces 'by' and 'eye' to go wholly unstressed. What you see and what you hear are not only not identical, but they cannot be brought into stereoscopic fusion save by the apprehending mind; Joyce said something similar of a detail from *Finnegans Wake*.

Here are new possibilities, facilitated by a machine that makes indentations and line-lengths exact – moreover makes all occurrences of the same word look *exactly* the same. With a typewriter on his desk, the poet is actually making something like what the reader of the printed page will look at, and poetry will not be the same again.

Nor, after about 1890, would the printed page be the same again. It would be typeset by machine as part of the mass-production of reading matter, going forward in England especially on the scale on which Henry Ford in America would one day mass-produce automobiles. Mergenthaler's first linotype patent was granted in 1885, the patent for its principal competitor the monotype in 1887. Before long the three-volume novel at 31*s*. 6*d*. gave way to the single-decker at 6*s*., compact enough to slip into an overcoat pocket for reading on a suburban train. Books had become time-killers for the steam- and electric-powered journeys on which middle-class commuters were spending much of their time, and the flourishing bookstalls were the ones in railway stations.

Here the crowd helps define an élite. One response to the mass-produced book was the 'difficult' book – *Prufrock and Other Observations*, *Ulysses*, the *Cantos* – and one response to the readership for the mass-produced book was a new élite which did not think of reading as a time-killer. Unlike former élites, this new élite was defined not by a social system but by self-selection. What did continue to be defined by a social system was apt to be the possession of money, and it was moneyed connoisseurs who purchased the other substitute for the mass-produced book. This was the 'fine' book, something on which craftsmanship had been lavished, beginning with the setting of type by hand. Next, sheets of good paper would be hand-fed into a hand-operated press, and there would be careful attention to details of binding. The edition would of course be 'limited', and the price high. The tradition of the 'fine' book in the modern era commences with the Kelmscott Press which William Morris founded in 1891 as a gesture of protest against machines in general.

It had the potentiality for a more precisely focused gesture than perhaps Morris knew, since the technology that made possible both the typewriter and the typesetting machine had been developed in the small-arms industry; the first typewriter with a shift-key for upper- and lower-case letters bore the name of Remington, the rifle-makers. As for the monotype, it employed both rifle technology and perforated paper borrowed from the Jacquard loom, emblem of the most satanic of mills. What a monstrosity, to have been midwifed by the gun-men and the mill-men in concert! A fiercer socialist than William Morris would have sharpened his attack. The 'aesthetic' protest of Morris ran toward the production of big, ornately unreadable editions of books one had already read, notably the Kelmscott Chaucer that the admirers of W. B. Yeats judged a worthy present for the poet's fortieth birthday (13 June 1905). The Morris tradition of craftsmanship was inherited by the Dun Emer, later the Cuala, Press, where the printing foreman, Emery Walker, had worked with Morris at Kelmscott, the typesetter and press-worker was W. B. Yeats's sister Elizabeth ('Lollie'), the literary adviser was W. B. Yeats himself, and the first offering, on 16 July 1903, was *In The Seven Woods, Being Poems Chiefly of the Irish Heroic Age*, by W. B. Yeats. The edition was limited to 325 copies, and cost 10*s*. 6*d*. for a mere 76 pages. On twice that money, in Dublin, you could live frugally for a week.

Unlike the Chaucer, *In the Seven Woods* was a 'new' book: new work, in fact, by Ireland's foremost poet. At that price, in that format, who bought it? Students of *Ulysses* may guess at a partial answer. The book's colophon, which tells us it was finished at Dundrum by Elizabeth Corbet Yeats 'the sixteenth day of July in the year of the big wind, 1903', is echoed by Buck Mulligan a little after eight in the morning of *Ulysses*. Mulligan glides from a mention of Dundrum to a jibe at a mock-book 'printed by the weird sisters in the year of the big wind' (*U* 13). On his next

appearance, about three in the afternoon, he refers to Stephen as
'Wandering Ængus' (*U* 249) ('Wandering Ængus of the Birds' is a
phrase from 'The Old Age of Queen Maeve'), and proceeds to
parody ten consecutive lines from 'Baile and Aillinn'. These
poems are no longer in the *Seven Woods* section of Yeats's *Collected
Poems*, but in 1903 they were, and at no other time. We may note
in fact that Mulligan's entire knowledge of Yeats, so far as he
displays it in *Ulysses*, is drawn from that one book, to the
colophon of which he reverts a few minutes before 11 p.m.; his
own 'British Beatitudes', he proposes, is to be 'printed and bound
at the Druiddrum Press by two designing females. Calf covers of
pissedon green. Last word in art shades. Most beautiful book
come out of Ireland my time' (*U* 424). It appears to have been
James Joyce's sour judgement that the destiny of such artefacts as
the Dun Emer Press manufactured was to pass into the possession
of elegant wastrels like Mulligan, to afford them occasions for
easy mockery.

This is an early example of a persistent theme, the continual
involvement of modernism with the technology and economics of
printing. Modernism's 'difficult' books were apt to be excluded
from systems of commercial publishing, and so found their way to
little presses where 'beautiful' books were a speciality. These
presses used hand-operated equipment that larger firms had
jettisoned in the course of modernizing, and they financed their
operations by selling to collectors who were not necessarily
readers. Pound's *Cantos I–XVI* (Three Mountains Press, Paris), his
Draft of XXX Cantos (Hours Press, Paris), Eliot's *Ara Vos Prec*
(Hogarth Press, London) and *Ulysses* itself (Shakespeare & Co.,
Paris) were all hand-set and hand-manufactured and available
chiefly to people who could afford them, and only by accident did
the public for a 'difficult' book and the public for a 'beautiful' one
at times partly coincide.

The private press with its finite stock of type serves too as
emblem for the deliberation writers were according to the
separate word and the separate letter. Never until the middle of
the nineteenth century had single words been the focus of so
much concentrated attention, philological, etymological, lexico-
graphical. The *OED* entry on the single word 'set' is two-thirds the
length of *Paradise Lost*. In 1882, the year of James Joyce's birth,
the last part of Skeat's *Etymological Dictionary* appeared, with

separate historical entries for many thousands of English words, traced wherever possible clear back to Indo-European roots. Joyce read in it 'by the hour'. Two years later the first fascicle (A–Ant) of the *OED* was published; that project ran until 1928, and when Joyce was working on 'Oxen of the Sun' about 1920 he used all of it (A–T) that then existed. Time and again a single word, like Chatterton's *akele*, would seize his attention; 'It is a good word,' he told Frank Budgen, 'and I shall probably use it.' *Tumultuary*, *difficultly*, *resiled*, were three rare words he used within a few lines to impart a flavour of Burke. Pound twice employed *satieties* as a token of Sappho; Eliot found *lacquearia* in Virgil and inserted it into *The Waste Land*, coined *polyphiloprogenitive* to fill by itself an octosyllabic line, and extracted special values from simple words like *dry*:

> Here I am, an old man in a dry month   ('Gerontion', 1)
>
> Dry bones can harm no one   (*The Waste Land*, V. 390)
>
> Dry the pool, dry concrete, brown edged
> ('Burnt Norton', I.36)
>
> The air which is now thoroughly small and dry.
> (*Ash-Wednesday*, I. 36)

Lexicography, storing, retrieving, assaying words, preceded word-processor technology by a century but already regarded language with the eye of such a technology. Other technologies foreran and fostered imaginative acts. The X-ray and its transparent planes helped prompt cubism. Marconi's waves in the ether made Donne's twisted eyebeams newly plausible. The careful labour of archaeologists gave minds a concrete, not an ideal, Troy, and at Minos uncovered a labyrinthine palace, at just about the time Orville and Wilbur Wright were fulfilling the ancient dream of mechanical wings. 'Stephen Dedalus', it is accurate to say, was a symbolic name made plausible by the concurrence of the Wrights with Sir Arthur Evans's Cretan excavations. One could learn about such matters in the illustrated papers that were published in large capital cities: in the *Illustrated London News*, for instance, which the new printing technologies enabled. Photo-engraving had only recently facilitated the reproduction of images in large cheap press runs.

Finally, as the new urban sensibility focused itself, its carrier from capital to capital was apt to be painting, which transcends language barriers. Music transcends them too, but considerable inertia attends the mobilization of avant-garde music: the hiring of halls and performers, the catching of the interest of conductors, the soothing of natural anxiety about what a paying public may be expected to tolerate. (Stravinsky's *Le Sacre*, the seeming exception, was ballet, not concert, music.)

This account could be much prolonged, and the more it was elaborated the more peculiar would seem the role of James Joyce. For if the modernism of 1910 and later answers to such a comprehensive description as I have been sketching, if it was a Gestalt of responses to the technology of a great modern city and the alterations effected by that technology in the quality of everyday urban life, then Joyce as arch-modernist seems unaccountable. His interest in painting was virtually nil, his interest in music intense but markedly old-fashioned: *The Bohemian Girl*, not *Le Sacre*. He grew up in a stagnant and impoverished city, up-to-date at the time he left only in its tram system. Dublin's sewage, even, was still emptied into the Liffey. And when he left Dublin it was not for London, like Pound and Eliot, nor for Paris, like Picasso and Stravinsky, but for a place as inconspicuous as Trieste. It is true that the more spectacular features of *Ulysses* were conceived only after he had settled for the first time in an up-to-date modern city, wartime Zürich, true that Zürich and then Paris appreciably accelerated his development. But it is also true that his development proceeded without discontinuity from principles we can discern in prose Joyce wrote in Dublin as early as 1904. If we agree with Fritz Senn that 'even in his earliest published prose Joyce wrote in a most complex, heavily allusive style, different from its later convoluted intricacies in *Ulysses* and *Finnegans Wake* in degree only',[7] then we concede the baffling fact that Joyce was a potential modernist before he left his native city at 22; the story Fritz Senn alludes to, 'The Sisters' which opens *Dubliners*, was written in Dublin and even published there, in the *Irish Homestead* for 13 August 1904, among advertisements for mineral waters and cream-separators. For the *Dubliners* version Joyce retouched the text extensively, but he did not feel, as other great modernists have felt, that very early work was to be discarded as incompatible with maturer work.

So Dublin's Joyce would seem to have entered the twentieth century by a different route, not the route of Hailey's Pound or St Louis's Eliot. As he did, because he was not a poet, in search of a mode of expression that felt right. He was a novelist, with a subject: something as old-fashioned as that. He had commenced to write about his subject while in Dublin. He took it with him into exile and continued to write about it. His devices, as they accreted by expressive necessity, gathered themselves around it. He found that he needed them for what he found himself needing to say.

The difference made by a subject, in Joyce's case a continuing, obsessive subject, deserves a little elaborating. The musician is not obligated by a 'subject'. He is driven by the need to write music, and if he is Stravinsky in 1911 he is driven too by the need to write the music of his own time, which shall be more than a paraphrase of existing music; hence *Le Sacre*. Picasso and Braque wanted to paint pictures of a certain order, pictures which should collapse the Renaissance tradition of three-dimensional illusion flat on to the picture plane. Hence 'cubist' pictures; and the 'subjects', frequently just things on table-tops, were secondary and nearly trivial. Poets, too, know what kind of poetry they want to write; the 'subject' is an occasion, sometimes an occasion sought. Like Milton listing possible themes for his *magnum opus*, Eliot and Pound may be discerned casting about for the contents of *The Waste Land* or the *Cantos*, having in the meantime kept busy perfecting their means of expression on lesser occasions. It is normal for all such artists to improve their command of means by constant exercise: to become, in the period we are scrutinizing, 'modernists', in advance of executing the work that shall absorb their most focal energies. But that was not Joyce's way. He became more and more deeply, more saliently 'modernist' in the course of writing what he had in him from the first to write about.

Joyce's subject began with the fact that he had been born in Rathgar, then Dublin's most prosperous suburb, eldest son of a substantial property owner, and was sent, before his sixth birthday, to Clongowes, the most fashionable boarding school in the keeping of the church's most prestigious teaching order; but by the time he was a college freshman the family for no clear reason was living in a slum, finishing breakfast consisted of draining a third cup of watery tea to the dregs, one crossed the city on foot to save penny tram-fares, and there was little to be done with one's BA save take it off to the continent to use in bargaining for a job teaching English to foreigners. His theme, in short, was catastrophic decline, from affluence to patched trousers in perhaps ten years. How had that happened, and to him? In what respects did it emblematize certain Irish realities, against which to measure the pretensions of political and cultural revival? And how – compensatory theme – had he survived to write about it?

His survival entailed the fact that he had not entered the priesthood, and this theme too deserves separate attention. If you were not going to drop into a clerkship, there were in general three things you could do with a college degree in Dublin. One was law. Joyce's friend Constantine P. Curran took that route. Another was medicine, the route travelled by his friend Oliver Gogarty, whose medical practice in time supported a literary career of distinguished amateurism. But the study of law and medicine took money, and though Joyce made a half-hearted attempt at medicine both his interest and his money ran out. The third option was the priesthood, which had been in Europe since the Middle Ages the recourse of the impecunious educated. One practical way in which it differs from law and medicine is that the church pays for your further studies, and one of the forces to impel James Joyce toward the seminary from a relatively early age was that he could have become something as distinguished as a Jesuit – 'the Reverend Stephen Dedalus, SJ' (P 161) – without imposing any further tax on his family's dwindling finances.

If these perspectives are less familiar than they might be, it is because the priesthood is not normally discussed as a possible solution to a career decision. One does not, by definition, choose to be a priest as one may choose to be a lawyer. The altar entails a vocation, which means a calling: one does not choose but is chosen, by God for the service of God. But any spiritual director will agree that appraising the reality of a vocation is a tricky thing entirely. ('You must be quite sure, Stephen, that you have a vocation,' says the director of studies in the *Portrait*, 'because it would be terrible if you found afterwards that you had none' (P 160).) There were indeed priests who had found that they had none, among them the old priest in the first story in *Dubliners*, 'The Sisters', who was discovered one night sitting in the dark in his confession-box, laughing softly. Joyce is careful to specify that when Stephen Dedalus discovered his appointed future 'A voice from beyond the world was calling' (*P* 167). So Art was indeed a vocation, and 'the inhuman voice that had called him to the pale service of the altar' (*P* 169) was merely the voice of the director of studies. 'Inhuman' is a word to be aware of; we are meant to reflect that the veritable voice of God would not be human either.

Joyce published hardly a sentence that does not offer some word to be aware of. 'There was no hope for him this time: it was the third stroke.' That is the first sentence in *Dubliners*, and it collects 'stroke' and 'time' into the same syntactic array, as though to acknowledge some sinister presiding clock. On the next page we find, 'Tiresome old fool! When we knew him first he used to be rather interesting, talking of faints and worms; but I soon grew tired of him and his endless stories about the distillery.' Faints and worms; swoons and death? No: 'faints', a plural without a singular, is the weaker stuff a distiller draws off and discards at the beginning and end of the run, and 'worms' are the coiled pipings in a still. Such words, we are being told, are no more locked to their common meanings than is the word 'stroke', which is one thing in the context of time and another in the context of the cardio-vascular system. Years later, when Joyce inserted into *Ulysses* an allusion to a book called *Ruby: A Novel Founded Upon Circus Life*, he amused himself with retitling it *Ruby: Pride of the Ring*, a phrase which, if you found it in *Finnegans Wake*, you'd not know whether to relate to circuses or to jewellery.

That clusterings and pairings of words, like faints/worms, like ruby/ring, can create phantom contexts which may be quite irrelevant to the context at hand was a discovery Joyce appears to have made on his own, aided by an early intentness upon words, by Skeat's *Etymological Dictionary*, and by analytic fascination with the ways of Dublin speech. It imparts to his least pretentious-looking prose an allusive density of the kind other writers have taught us to designate 'modernist', long before we are made to discern it rampant in the *Wake*, where among our other difficulties we are never sure which context ought to govern at the moment. Thus if we search the story called 'Grace' for the word 'grace', we find it here:

Mr Kernan was a commercial traveller of the old school which believed in the dignity of its calling. He had never been seen in the city without a silk hat of some decency and a pair of gaiters. By grace of these two articles of clothing, he said, a man could always pass muster.[8]

There is 'grace', and near it is 'believed', and near it too is 'calling': vocation. Bishops, for that matter, are the usual wearers of 'gaiters'. And how are we to take 'of some decency' (exercise: visualize a hat of less decency than that), and what is 'pass muster'? The passage bristles with curiosities.

'Pass muster' is one thing we can gloss. 'Muster' is from Latin *monstrare*, to show, whence also 'monster', something shown. Troops were 'mustered', put on show for inspection; you passed muster if the officer saw nothing wrong with your dress. Being Mr Kernan's own phrase, 'pass muster' has overtones of jocular camaraderie, but companion words in Joyce's sentences tug its military context toward St Paul's injunction that we put on the armour of God to stand against the Devil. It is not surprising that, when a somewhat rehabilitated Mr Kernan makes his appearance at church, both he and the author pay some attention to the hat.

His hat, which had been rehabilitated by his wife, rested upon his knees. Once or twice he pulled down his cuffs with one hand while he held the brim of his hat lightly, but firmly, with the other hand.[9]

(Note the double commas setting off 'but firmly'; that is a markedly *firm* firmness.)

Among these details we should distinguish two orders of precision, one of them traditional but the other distinctly modernist. What is traditional is the intention registered by the placing of the commas around 'but firmly'. This acknowledges the oldest order of fictional mimesis, the narrating voice, and tells us exactly what that voice is doing. The storyteller's voice is making an ironic point, by vocal inflection. That was the way Dickens, for instance, made ironic points, and a Dickens paragraph on the page is a score for our own reading voice, which whether we read aloud or silently supplies us with our substantial experience of the storyteller's voice, a voice we hear by listening to ourselves. Writers like musicians for a century now have tended to guide the voice by explicit notation, of which Joyce's care with commas is an instance. We need not wonder that he so objected to having his pointing regularized in publishers' offices, or that getting it, so far as possible, restored has constituted, in the presently available editions of *Dubliners* and the *Portrait*, a major enterprise for textual scholarship.

But in the other effects we have been examining, we perceive a modernist's attention to dimensions of language beyond the reach of the expressive voice. 'Mr Kernan was a commercial traveller of the old school . . .': return to that quotation, and observe how its clusterings of diction – 'believed', 'calling', 'decency', 'grace', 'gaiters' – associate in independence of anything the voice can do. There is no way of reading the paragraph that will bring forward, without archness, the community these words find in religious discourse. The voice attends to the main narrative line, on which they denote a merely sartorial, and scruffily sartorial, decorum. So our apprehending mind must be active on two planes, attending to a narrative voice that is telling us, without special emphasis, about a few mannerisms of Mr Kernan's, and attending simultaneously to a little luminous cloud that is generated by the diction arrayed on the page. Like the Marianne Moore stanza that employs its lineation to point up rhymes the reading voice cannot emphasize, these Joyce sentences employ semantic affinities to impose a formality the narrative cannot quite acknowledge. The words are combining according to two different intentions, and the storyteller, whose ministrations a reading voice can imitate, is responsible for only one of them.

It can be helpful to personify the second intention, which tends to stand aloof and pare its finger-nails. Confronting a similar duality in *Ulysses*, David Hayman some years ago had us imagine someone he called the Arranger, responsible for patterns that transcend normal narrative inflections: the captions for instance that interrupt the narrative in 'Aeolus', or the parodies that interrupt it in 'Cyclops'.

'Cyclops' is an enlightening case to examine: for the most part a *tour de force* of spoken narrative, so scrupulous with mannerisms of speech it calls for performance, and for adequate performance an expert command of the lower Dublin accents:

But that's the most notorious bloody robber you'd meet in a

day's walk and the face on him all pockmarks would hold a shower of rain. *Tell him*, says he, *I dare him*, says he, *and I doubledare him to send you round here again or if he does*, says he, *I'll have him summonsed up before the court, so will I, for trading without a licence.* And he after stuffing himself till he's fit to burst! Jesus, I had to laugh at the little jewy getting his shirt out. *He drink me my teas. He eat me my sugars. Because he no pay me my moneys?* (*U* 292)

This wants a dropping inflection at the end of each sentence, and attention to such details as the vowel in 'Jesus' (Jaysus) or the rhyming of 'bloody' with 'moody', not with 'goody'. It wants, too, a command of three voices, the narrator's, the 'bloody robber''s, the 'little jewy''s. It lays richly on the page the mimetic Dublin way of telling a story, and to hear it in accomplished Irish performance is a treat.

But neither the accomplished Irish performer nor anyone else can find a voice for Joyce's very next sentences, because they do not exist for speaking:

For nonperishable goods bought of Moses Herzog, of 13 Saint Kevin's parade, Wood quay ward, merchant, hereinafter called the vendor, and sold and delivered to Michael E. Geraghty, Esquire, of 29 Arbour Hill in the city of Dublin, Arran quay ward, gentleman, hereinafter called the purchaser, videlicet, five pounds avoirdupois of first choice tea at three shillings per pound avoirdupois. (*U* 292–3)

This legal document is something inertly *written*. It lies on the page as though pasted there, and the performing voice has no recourse save to skip over it.

It was for interruptions of this order that Professor Hayman found it helpful to invoke the Arranger, a name seemingly prompted by their air of existing in printed space, not in speaking time. But the supra-vocal patterns we were observing in the diction of 'Grace' have that kind of spatial existence too, and having observed this we note the corollary, that a proto-Arranger was in Joyce's repertory as early as 1906, when he wrote 'Grace' at the age of 24. At work on 'Cyclops' a dozen years later, he foregrounded discontinuities in a way casual observers never fail to call 'modernist'; but the methods of 'Cyclops' were not summoned out of nowhere by modernist fiat but evolved in easy stages from those of *Dubliners*.

So what was he up to in *Dubliners*? The answer is not that he was trying to be 'modern', whatever that would have meant in 1904–6. He was working on a principle to which he afforded a clue in the *Stephen Hero* manuscript of the same period, where, after being told that Stephen read in Skeat's *Etymological Dictionary* 'by the hour', we next learn how 'People seemed to him strangely ignorant of the value of the words they used so glibly.' That strange ignorance underlies many of Joyce's precisions. 'By grace of these two articles of clothing, he said': we are meant to hear Mr Kernan saying 'grace' in strange ignorance of *gratia*, something freely given and normally given by God. As an adult convert to Catholicism he would have been told this, but the telling did not register. It was by the city's semantic traps, Joyce thought, that such decline as his family's had been abetted.

One more example from 'Grace':

> The transept of the Jesuit Church in Gardiner Street was almost full; and still at every moment gentlemen entered from the side-door and, directed by the lay-brother, walked on tiptoe along the aisles until they found seating accommodation.[10]

'Gentlemen' is one key word, a recurrent word in 'Grace', in fact its very first noun ('Two gentlemen who were in the lavatory at the time'). At present being a gentleman entails knowing to walk on tiptoe if you have entered church late. No longer denoting someone 'entitled to bear arms, though not ranking among the nobility' (*OED*), the word has completed its dreary transit toward the merely genteel. But in its proteiform uses of 'gentleman' the story has made this point already. What is novel about the sentence we set out to examine is its ending: 'until they found seating accommodation.' Why did the economical Joyce not write 'until they found seats'?

They found seating accommodation, we may next reflect, because that was what they were looking for: not mere space to sit in. 'Seating accommodation' would be their kind of phrase in this kind of place, a fumble after polysyllabic elegance.[11]

But there is more. 'Accommodation', as it happens, is one more word with a religious history. The *OED*'s second sense is

'Adaptation of a word, expression or system to something different from its original purpose'. This is backed up by three quotations which all pertain to doctrinal watering-down. We notice that Father Purdon's sermon is, by that definition, a most accommodating performance. 'He told his hearers that he was there that evening for no terrifying, no extravagant purpose; but as a man of the world speaking to his fellow-men.' Accommodation, yes, that is what the gentlemen have all come for, who would not otherwise have come; it begins with seating accommodation, and extends to moral and doctrinal. And if the storyteller has so managed his tale as to make this thoroughly apparent, he has been abetted by the Arranger, who has made the least of verbal minutiae fit into his tight mosaic.

This habit of patterning the diction of whole passages is familiar to readers of the later Joyce, who may tend to think it whimsical extravagance. Familiar examples include (my italics) the food words sprinkled like salt over 'Lestrygonians' – 'Muslin prints, silk, dames and dowagers, jingle of harnesses, hoofthuds lowringing in the *baking* causeway' (*U* 168) – the winds in 'Aeolus' – 'Just this ad, Mr Bloom said, pushing through towards the steps, *puffing*, and taking the cutting from his pocket' (*U* 146) – or the musical terms in 'Sirens', where Miss Kennedy '*transposed* the teatray' (*U* 258) and Miss Douce the barmaid 'with *grace* . . . tapped a *measure* of gold whiskey' (*U* 261). In *Finnegans Wake* the method runs rampant. The famous river names by the hundred that bubble through the twenty pages of 'Anna Livia Plurabelle' afford merely the most celebrated instance. Any passage you can point to is stitched with analogous consistencies.

> When, pressures be to our hoary frother, the pop gave his sullen bulletaction and, bilge, sled a movement of catharic emulsipotion down the sloppery slide of a slaunty to tilted lift-ye-landsmen. (*FW* 310.35–311.1)

Uncorking a bottle of Bass, we are to understand, is a sacred rite; hence (praises be to our Holy Father) the Pope gave his solemn benediction; Catholic Emancipation is our toast (as a sub-theme it unites 'movement' and 'cathartic'), complete with a Gaelic *Slainté*! ('Your health!').

The mere look of that sentence assures us that we are well into the twentieth century (it was written about 1936). But at no point can Joyce be discerned deciding to cast off his tame ways and write in the manner of the brave new century: in Pound's phrase, to modernize himself. What is discernible instead is the slow and deliberate evolution of that duality between narrative and diction he had devised for *Dubliners*, with the aid of Skeat, as a mimetic and diagnostic device. Everything Joyce did, every extravagance of his later manner, is traceable to that and to his other major innovation, the multiplane narrative. This, though implicit in the *Dubliners* separation between storyteller and word-arranger, is developed and foregrounded for the first time in the book that gave Joyce more trouble per page than any other, *A Portrait of the Artist as a Young Man*.

The *Dubliners* stories were about Dublin paralysis. The *Portrait* was about his second theme, his own emergence from the paralysed city. Who could tell that story? Only he could. But how? No 'I' that tells can be the 'me' that is told of. First-person narrative would not be feasible, and that the *Bildungsroman* should be in the third person was a very early decision. But that implies an omniscient observer, ideally a book written by God. There were months and years of impasse.

Though when and how it was written we do not know, the first page of the final *Portrait* is arguably the twentieth century's most radically innovative single literary gesture, notwithstanding that it begins 'Once upon a time'.

> Once upon a time and a very good time it was there was a moocow coming down along the road and this moocow that was coming down along the road met a nicens little boy named baby tuckoo. . . .
>
> His father told him that story: his father looked at him through a glass: he had a hairy face.
>
> He was baby tuckoo. The moocow came down the road where Betty Byrne lived: she sold lemon platt.
>
> > *O, the wild rose blossoms*
> > *On the little green place.*
>
> He sang that song. That was his song.
>
> > *O, the green wothe botheth.* (*P* 7)

Not until the syntactic hiccup 'and this moocow' can a new reader be sure that the first sentence is mimetic, not narrative: that it does not present a moocow with the aid of immemorial conventions but imitates a pompous voice, condescending ('nicens') while loving.

'His father told him that story': that at least resembles the accent of the familiar omniscient narrator. But there is more to the sentence, a three-parted affair with colons at the joints. 'His father told him that story: his father looked at him through a glass: he had a hairy face.' It is on the second clause that everything hinges, since in substituting 'glass' for the fancier 'monocle' it adapts the eight-word sequence to a child's vocabulary, hence to the child's viewpoint. So 'His father told him that story' is not the narrator stating, but the child remembering, in a narrative that keeps the child at just the small equivocal distance that a transformation from first person to third can signal. These are delicate distinctions indeed.

So delicate are they that the next sentence, 'He was baby tuckoo', is not the same kind of sentence as 'He was Stephen Dedalus', despite the identical form. Rather, 'He was baby tuckoo' reflects his realization that the story he is (was?) hearing is (was?) about him: like the story we are reading. Then:

> *O, the wild rose blossoms*
> *On the little green place.*

He sang that song. That was his song.

> *O, the green wothe botheth.*

This especially solicits the fit readers though few who can recognize in 'place' a parental substitution for 'grave'. (Not to tell us some things if we happen not to know them is not only a modernist pedagogy, it inheres in the logic of this page, which can impart nothing the child does not know.) What a song, what a family, what a country! And who is it that has supplied the phonetic transcription of how 'he' sang it, on a page otherwise free of such deformations? Is the boy remembering, or reliving, or what? Or is he a creation merely of these simple words? If so, he is a nearly Euclidean construct, the pages being laid out as though with a T-square, and the vocabulary of non-redundant economy. It all exists in the domain of the Arranger, who has never before done such intricate, delicate work, a little textbook of creative discontinuities. The quick cutting of *The Waste Land* is foreshadowed here. It may date from as early as 1909.

We speak of the Arranger to avoid speaking of that troublesome person, the Narrator. 'Person', Joyce seems to have decided early on, is a grammatical fiction. The statement 'Jack kissed Jill' creates three persons, Jack and Jill and whoever is affirming. But if no one is audible, if the sentence simply lies before us in print? Then the writer, the Arranger, some such phantom person must be invoked, in full awareness that he is phantasmal, a residuum of the logic grammar entails. If we knew that the sentence had been arranged by a computer the arrangement would still be haunted by that phantom.

> Woodshadows floated silently by through the morning peace from the stairhead seaward where he gazed. Inshore and farther out the mirror of water whitened, spurned by lightshod hurrying feet. White breast of the dim sea. The twining stresses, two by two. A hand plucking the harpstrings merging their twining chords. Wavewhite wedded words shimmering on the dim tide.   (*U* 9)

Who narrates this, on an early page of *Ulysses*? By the thirtieth word we may forget we asked; 'White breast of the dim sea' is Stephen recalling a quotation, the rest seems interior monologue, Stephen trying out phrases, outdoing Yeats. But what about the first two sentences, with their 'lightshod hurrying feet'? In form they are 'narrative' sentences, in diction Stephen's: 'lightshod hurrying feet' seems out of character for a narrator who has hereto been content with unmemorable lines like 'He walked off quickly round the parapet' (*U* 9). Yet it makes little sense for Stephen to be composing past-tense narrative, and we may want to say that Stephen is being written about in a style he would approve, or else that, like 'He was baby tuckoo', these sentences exist in an equivocal domain, somewhere between Stephen and the Arranger. 'Lightshod', by the way: lightly shod, or shod with light? Those ideal feet resemble the fingers of Homer's famous dawn, and it seems pertinent to ask whether Homer's shade, even, hovers hereabouts, sponsoring all those compounds: 'wavewhite', 'lightshod', 'woodshadows'.

Clearly, there is no simple answer to any question we may raise about narrative authority; there has been none ever since the *Portrait* installed the mind of the text in that narrow equivocal space between Arranger and Stephen. That was a step the *Portrait* took as *Dubliners* took the step of doubling storyteller and

Arranger, and for similar practical and mimetic reasons. It helped solve the problems of writing a novel out of material drawn from one's less mature self.

For one's less mature self understood less: hence the need for a system of expressive limits. This is what Joyce came to mean by a style: a set of mannerisms defined by what it cannot say.

> And he felt the prefect's hand on his forehead; and he felt his forehead warm and damp against the prefect's cold damp hand. That was the way a rat felt, slimy and damp and cold. Every rat had two eyes to look out of. Sleek slimy coats, little little feet tucked up to jump, black shiny eyes to look out of. They could understand how to jump. But the minds of rats could not understand trigonometry. When they were dead they lay on their sides. Their coats dried then. They were only dead things.
>
> (P 22)

That rats cannot understand trigonometry is a truth seldom inscribed, so it is incorrect to say that this style is confined to the obvious. Still, in its simplicities, its transitions from the concrete to the concrete, its seeming innocence of synonyms, its adherence to short declarative structures compounded but never subordinated, it is a style that declares its limitations also: a style that thinks like a serious little boy, and not a style in which to qualify or seek out nuances.

The famous 'styles' of *Ulysses* build on this principle: they are systems of exclusion. 'Gerty just took off her hat for a moment to settle her hair and a prettier, a daintier head of nutbrown tresses was never seen on a girl's shoulders, a radiant little vision, in sooth, almost maddening in its sweetness' (*U* 360): that too is no style in which to make discriminations, though Gerty would have us know that, ah, *she* discriminates. Similarly the style that narrates an execution –

> The learned prelate who administered the last comforts of holy religion to the hero martyr when about to pay the death penalty knelt in a most christian spirit in a pool of rainwater, his cassock above his hoary head, and offered up to the throne of grace fervent prayers of supplication   (*U* 308–9)

– whatever this can express (what?) it is not a style capable of admitting to the sheer brutality of what is going on.

And if style is limitation, style is the mimetic principle that will distinguish character from character: character is limitation too, and Bloom is not Stephen.

> That brought us out of the land of Egypt and into the house of bondage. Something in all those superstitions because when you go out never know what dangers. Hanging on to a plank or astride of a beam for grim life, lifebelt round round him, gulping salt water, and that's the last of his nibs till the sharks catch hold of him. Do fish ever get seasick? (*U* 378–9)

That can only be Bloom. And that is only an arrangement of words. No, there is no Bloom. There is language.

* * *

Nor is there any Dublin either: there is language. And the phantom persons created by that language – including, as we have seen, such phantoms as we are to imagine arranging the language – are responsible for the unique perception of the city that Joyce's labyrinthine methods create. Nowhere are the deep connections between modernism and modern urban rhythms more evident: not in *Manhattan Transfer*, not in *Mrs Dalloway*, not even in the German expressionist cinema. Joyce applied his powers throughout his life to the increasingly complex evocation of the city, one city, Dublin. His powers developed with his progressive absorption in this theme, and the final evocations of the city in *Finnegans Wake* effectively sunder the liaison with Milton's Pandemonium which had made of the city an equivocal infernal place for a quarter of a millennium. It may be claimed of Joyce that he reinvented the city for literature, and that *Paradise Lost*, as a source of imaginative paradigms, has now in effect been supplanted by *Ulysses*.

To appraise with any justice his dealings with Dublin, we must commence by exorcizing one of Joyce's best-known *obiter dicta*, the famous statement, in the letter to Grant Richards, that Dublin was 'the centre of Irish paralysis' (*Letters*, II. 134). That expresses one level of the complex feelings he brought to the composition of *Dubliners*, a young man's book dating chiefly from 1904–6. What it leaves unstated is what Joyce regarded as a larger truth, that the paralysis, like the snow in 'The Dead', was 'general all over Ireland'. Whatever Irish qualities might be discernible anywhere,

Dublin was their centre. To deem otherwise is to interpret Joyce's feelings about his city with the aid of the very Miltonic stereotypes his life-work has had the effect of dissipating: to assume for instance with Yeats that if there was corruption in Dublin there was purity in Galway, or with J. M. Synge that there was squalor in Dublin as in Paris, but vitality in the remote islands. A principal reason for the undoubted fact that the leaders of the Irish Revival found Joyce unassimilable, while he for his part thought them in league with the trolls and the rabblement, was that Joyce, a city man to his bones, confronted literati whose deepest values derived from pastoral romance.

Thus, though Yeats was born in Dublin his heart was in Sligo; Dublin was 'this unmannerly town', characterized by its 'daily spite', by shopkeepers whose occupation was to 'fumble in a greasy till' and to 'add the halfpence to the pence' ('September 1913', 2–3).[12] It was the place where they rioted at the Abbey, where they did not want the Lane pictures, where they hooted (as he supposed) John Synge to his death. Its 'pavements grey' ('The Lake Isle', 11) were indistinguishable from London's, where one might guard one's sanity by dreaming of a lake isle. A man for whom one might want to write a poem was no Dubliner but a level-eyed fly-fisherman,

> A man who does not exist,
> A man who is but a dream;

and the poem you would hope to write for him would be

> maybe as cold
> And passionate as the dawn.

('The Fisherman', 35–6; 39–40)

Synge too was Dublin-born, and thought the city congested with thick-necked sweaty-headed swine. Man, he thought, 'is intellectually a nomad, and all wanderers have finer intellectual and physical perceptions than men who are condemned to local habitations.'[13] He signed his letters to his sweetheart 'Your old Tramp', and was never happier than on the road. He and Yeats came repeatedly to the Big House, Coole, which Lady Gregory maintained near Gort in Galway, far away west from the Nelson Pillar and the Dublin trams. In a Big House, comfortably shut away from the urban yet surrounded by amenities not indigenous to the rural, one might dream that the soul of Ireland was alight among turf fires on peasant hearths. *Ulysses* condenses their doctrine in words it assigns to George Russell ('AE'):

> The movements which work revolution in the world are born out of the dreams and visions in a peasant's heart on the hillside. For them the earth is not an exploitable ground but the living mother. The rarefied air of the academy and the arena produce the sixshilling novel, the musichall song. France produces the finest flower of corruption in Mallarmé, but the desirable life is revealed only to the poor of heart, the life of Homer's Phaeacians.   (*U* 186–7)

The poor of heart, approached by a touring enquirer, are apt to give voice to the supposition that 'there must be terrible queer creatures at the latter end of the world' (*P* 251), and when Joyce has Stephen Dedalus write the anecdote of such an encounter in his diary, he also has Stephen append his reflections on the old man who spoke those words:

> I fear him. I fear his redrimmed horny eyes. It is with him I must struggle all through this night till day come, till he or I lie dead, gripping him by the sinewy throat till . . . Till what? Till he yield to me? No. I mean him no harm.   (*P* 252)

Peasant ignorance, when it passes for peasant wisdom, seems to Stephen a monstrosity to be feared. Fear, hate: these are, Stephen comes to recognize, excessive responses; but they were conceived on Stephen's behalf by James Joyce out of the wariness with which he scrutinized the Revival. 'An aesthete', he wrote of Yeats, 'has a floating will', and Yeats brought to his task of revitalizing poetry both the conventional pastoral values of English Romanticism and an easy willingness to accept the values of AE, a man from a village, and George Moore, a man from a western estate: two men profoundly out of sympathy with the special potentialities of Dublin.

Some of these potentialities are caught in isolated passages of *Dubliners*, a book which elsewhere seems dedicated to the programme of displaying Dublin as a city of traps. Here is the opening paragraph of 'Two Gallants':

> The grey warm evening of August had descended upon the city and a mild warm air, a memory of summer, circulated in the streets. The streets, shuttered for the repose of Sunday,

swarmed with a gaily coloured crowd. Like illumined pearls the lamps shone from the summits of their tall poles upon the living texture below which, changing shape and hue unceasingly, sent up into the warm grey evening air an unchanging unceasing murmur.[14]

Like so many paragraphs in *A Portrait of the Artist as a Young Man*, this passage circles back to its beginning, from 'the grey warm evening' and 'mild warm air' of its opening clauses to the 'warm grey evening air' of its finale. Latterly the crowd, 'changing shape and hue unceasingly', sends up 'an unchanging unceasing murmur'. 'Murmur', a word built on a repetition, concentrates many acoustic repetitions: the doubled 'warm' of the first sentence, the juxtaposed 'streets . . . streets' at the juncture of the first and second, the chained alliterations ('city', 'summer', 'circulated', 'streets', 'streets', 'shuttered', 'Sunday', 'swarmed', 'shone', 'summits', 'shape', 'unceasingly', 'sent', 'unceasing') that stitch the whole. The one simile makes the lamps 'like illumined pearls'; the one metaphor makes the crowd 'a living texture', a phrase that remembers the tactility of 'texture': by derivation, something *woven*, like a text. Beneath such carefully muted lyricism we discern no judgement that the city is such a bad place to be alive in.

In *Ulysses* it is in Bloom's company that we are introduced to the city, for instance in such a passage as the following, where he is looking for a safe place to read his *poste restante* letter:

He turned into Cumberland street and, going on some paces, halted in the lee of the station wall. No-one. Meade's timberyard. Piled balks. Ruins and tenements. With careful tread he passed over a hopscotch court with its forgotten pickeystone. Not a sinner. Near the timberyard a squatted child at marbles, alone, shooting the taw with a cunnythumb. A wise tabby, a blinking sphinx, watched from her warm sill.

(*U* 77)

Here we are commencing to encounter the staccato rhythms of Joyce's maturity, derived, yes, from the mimetic abruptness of the interior monologue, but engaged also in the notation of urban variety. You turn a corner, and instantly a new cityscape: here ruins and litter, appropriated by children for hopscotch and marbles. Children, not being trained to regard squalor as squalor, see possibility in variousness everywhere, and their special vocabulary – 'pickeystone', 'taw', 'cunnythumb' – squares variousness and cubes it. The tabby cat presides, exotic, 'a blinking sphinx'. Her sill is 'warm'. This is the kind of vista Yeats would have hated, and AE would not have thought it fit to paint. Joyce's presentation contains no hint of revulsion.

An episode later, and we are being taken across Dublin very rapidly by coach. Places appear in cinematic flicker:

> Dead side of the street this. Dull business by day, land agents, temperance hotel, Falconer's railway guide, civil service college, Gill's, catholic club, the industrious blind. Why? Some reason. Sun or wind. At night too. Chummies and slaveys. Under the patronage of the late Father Mathew. Foundation stone for Parnell. Breakdown. Heart.   (*U* 95)

'Dead side of the street' and 'Breakdown. Heart' enclose this because we are in 'Hades', the funeral episode. What they enclose, though, is the poetry of the list, a poetic much developed in *Ulysses*: a book itself founded, as Richard Kain discovered and Clive Hart has confirmed in detail, on the alphabetized lists of *Thom's Dublin Directory*. With an eye on *Thom's*, Joyce is moving us north up Sackville Street.

Writing itself originated, apparently, from the need to record lists, which are difficult to remember. These were the lists appropriate to urban organization: taxgatherers' rolls, storehouse inventories. City directories were a later development, the grid of the streets and the numbering of the houses prompting a filing system for what wayfarers might encounter, and Joyce pored over *Thom's* as over a sacred book. It has two main sorts of list, cross-referenced: alphabetical by person, with address appended; sequentially along the street, with persons' names appended. The latter were the ones Joyce found most useful. They helped him with verisimilitude (he installed the Blooms in a house on Eccles Street which, according to *Thom's*, was empty in 1904), and they afforded models for such a rhetoric as we have been examining: 'land agents, temperance hotel, Falconer's railway guide, civil service college, Gill's, catholic club, the industrious blind.' These are sequential establishments, the sequence epitomizing urban variety.

The opening of the next episode deserves transcription *in extenso*:

IN THE HEART OF THE HIBERNIAN METROPOLIS

Before Nelson's Pillar trams slowed, shunted, changed trolley, started for Blackrock, Kingstown and Dalkey, Clonskea, Rathgar and Terenure, Palmerston park and upper Rathmines, Sandymount Green, Rathmines, Ringsend and Sandymount Tower, Harold's Cross. The hoarse Dublin United Tramway Company's timekeeper bawled them off:

—Rathgar and Terenure!

—Come on, Sandymount Green!

Right and left parallel clanging ringing a doubledecker and a singledeck moved from their railheads, swerved to the down line, glided parallel.

—Start, Palmerston park!

THE WEARER OF THE CROWN

Under the porch of the general post office shoeblacks called and polished. Parked in North Prince's street His Majesty's vermilion mailcars, bearing on their sides the royal initials, E.R., received loudly flung sacks of letters, postcards, lettercards, parcels, insured and paid, for local, provincial, British and overseas delivery.

GENTLEMEN OF THE PRESS

Grossbooted draymen rolled barrels dullthudding out of Prince's stores and bumped them up on the brewery float. On the brewery float bumped dullthudding barrels rolled by grossbooted draymen out of Prince's stores.   (*U* 116)

By now we are immersed in the veritable urban clang and bustle, yet the rhetoric is extending itself according to tried principles. Lists are in evidence: the first paragraph is a list of tramlines; a later paragraph lists various categories of mail. The barrels, one senses, are not listed, because they are identical, but the sentence that moves them from the stores to the brewery float repeats itself, element by element, in reverse order like a strip of film scanned this way first, then that.

And the captions bespeak not only urban newspapers but urban discontinuities: a blatant new claim, each few minutes, on our attention. And the wording of those claims: does 'HEART' mean 'heart'? Are those trams corpuscular entities? Is that timekeeper the pacemaker? And 'The Wearer of the Crown', how exactly is he here? Do those mailcars personify him? And what about the 'Gentlemen of the Press'? They will be introduced a few lines after the above quotation stops, but meanwhile are we to think of them as barrel-rollers, as narcotic-distributors? (Those barrels contain porter.)

This is a disorienting page indeed, and yet a lively page. Liveliness, that has been so far the note of Joyce's sense of the city, from 'Two Gallants' clear to 'Aeolus' in *Ulysses*. The rhythms have grown more abrupt, the tempi more barbaric, the glimpsing more evidently syncopated, but the note of vitality, extending even to the author's incentive to find expressive devices, is unmistakable. This is powerful cumulative evidence to be weighed against the city details in the next episode, 'Lestry-gonians', where narrative spirits are depressed because Bloom is depleted.

> Cityful passing away, other cityful coming, passing away too: other coming on, passing on. Houses, lines of houses, streets, miles of pavements, piledup bricks, stones. Changing hands. This owner, that. . . . Piled up in cities, worn away age after age. Pyramids in sand. Built on bread and onions. Slaves. Chinese wall. Babylon. Big stones left. Round towers. Rest rubble, sprawling suburbs, jerrybuilt, Kerwan's mushroom houses, built of breeze. Shelter for the night.   (*U* 164)

This, in a much-anthologized detail of *Ulysses*, is the infernal city of Blake and of Milton, an empty transience where 'No one is anything' (*U* 164). Bloom's next words are less often transcribed:

> This is the very worst hour of the day. Vitality. Dull, gloomy. Hate this hour.   (*U* 164)

That would appear to be Joyce's judgement on the facile negativism we have learned to parrot about cities. What we need in that mood, thinks Bloom, is a decent meal.

A decent meal, though, assuming he has had it, did not improve the temper of the narrating consciousness of 'Wandering Rocks', that synchronized panoramic jump-cut view of a whole city, physical, moral, commercial. It opens, 'The superior', which we take to be an adjective until later words force us to reassess it as a noun: 'The superior, the very reverend John Conmee S.J., reset his smooth watch' (*U* 219); and we think we know what it means to reset a watch until more words force yet another reassessment: 'reset his smooth watch in his interior pocket as he came down the presbytery steps' (*U* 219). Here discontinuities have invaded the very sentence, the syntax of perception itself requiring frequent compensatory attentions. 'The viceroy was most cordially greeted on his way through the metropolis' (*U* 252), we read as though in a Unionist paper. Then we read, 'On Ormond quay Mr Simon Dedalus, steering his way from the greenhouse for the subsheriff's office, stood still in midstreet and brought his hat low. His Excellency graciously returned Mr Dedalus' greeting' (*U* 252). This seems an instant of loyal cordiality until we reflect that Mr Dedalus is no conspicuous loyalist, that he is 'steering his way' having spent some time imbibing in the Scotch House, that a 'greenhouse' is a public urinal, and that the lowered placement of his hat very possibly reflects uncertainty as to whether he has buttoned his fly. The greeting His Excellency returned was never given; nor was the greeting the casual reader perceived.

The city is extended in space and replete with empty synchronies of time. Thus the fate of a discarded handbill riding Liffey currents incurs exactly as close attention as any other fates:

> A skiff, a crumpled throwaway, Elijah is coming, rode lightly down the Liffey, under Loopline bridge, shooting the rapids where water chafed around the bridgepiers, sailing eastward past hulls and anchorchains, between the Customhouse old dock and George's quay. (*U* 227)

Later:

> North wall and sir John Rogerson's quay, with hulls and anchorchains, sailing westward, sailed by a skiff, a crumpled throwaway, rocked on the ferry-wash, Elijah is coming. (*U* 240)

Later still:

> Elijah, skiff, crumpled throwaway, sailed eastward by flanks of ships and trawlers, amid an archipelago of corks, beyond new Wapping street past Benson's ferry, and by the threemasted schooner *Rosevean* from Bridgwater with bricks. (*U* 249)

So the current moves, and so a crumpled handbill moves, now east, now west, delayed by eddies. So too people move, and behold, on one page the onelegged sailor is near Mountjoy Square, and on another is turning into Eccles Street, and on yet another is at 14 Nelson Street. The same omniscient camera eye that picked up the throwaway picks him up, as it picks up too on another page 'a darkbacked figure under Merchant's arch' (*U* 227) scanning books on the hawker's car. A few pages later two walkers, Lenehan and M'Coy, going 'down the steps and under Merchant's arch', notice that darkbacked figure: it is Bloom.

—Wonder what he is buying, M'Coy said, glancing behind.
—*Leopoldo or the Bloom is on the Rye*, Lenehan said. (*U* 233)

Two pages later we are shown Mr Bloom scanning books, dealing with a rheumy shopkeeper, responding to and selecting *Sweets of Sin*; unless we are very alert we may not notice that, though still a darkbacked figure, he is no longer at a hawker's cart, but in a nondescript shop whose proprietor keeps the salacious stock behind a curtain. For appearances deceive; what we glimpsed before may not be what we see in close-up now. A city is a place of quick glances, misleading correlations, illusion.

For an hour of book time (more precisely, 65 minutes) Joyce detains us in this labyrinth, doing nothing to solace our discomfort as we strive to locate ourselves, locate our characters, connect glimpse with glimpse or name with name, and sometimes determine that they are not connectible. The Mr Bloom of 'Mr Bloom's dental windows' (*U* 250) beneath which Cashel Boyle O'Connor Fitzmaurice Tisdall Farrell collided with the blind stripling is not the Bloom we know but an otherwise non-signifying dentist named Marcus Bloom, and if we thought otherwise we too incur the stripling's curse:

—God's curse on you, he said sourly, whoever you are! You're blinder nor I am, you bitch's bastard!   (*U* 250)

The blind man, in this strange city, is our surrogate. (Exercise: attempt to define 'bitch's bastard'.)

This is the city as labyrinth, the city as array of facing mirrors, the city defined by precisely delineated contours set in unsettling relations. It is not, though, despite its deep inhospitality, Milton's Infernal City. Nothing beckons like the infernal; this city does not beckon. It is a city like Homer's or Joshua Slocum's high seas, where one must navigate and compute, subject continually to observational and computational error. (You can read a sextant to a tenth of a minute, which is a six-hundredth of a degree. But this accuracy is delusional since you must correct for refraction, and the corrections entail a residue of approximation. They depend, for example, upon ambient temperature, and upon such things as scatter caused by recent volcanic eruptions.)

'Thus the unfacts, did we possess them,' *Finnegans Wake* admonishes, 'are too imprecisely few to warrant our certitude' (*FW* 57.16–17), and what with 'tramtrees, fargobawlers, auto-kinotons, hippohobbilies, streetfleets, tournintaxes' (*FW* 5.31–2), not to mention 'the fumes and the hopes and the strupithump of his ville's indigenous romekeepers, homesweepers, dome-creepers' (*FW* 6.3–5), we may be perpetually uncertain what exactly it is we are being shown: whether for instance the 'skysign of soft advertisement' (*FW* 4.13–14) is Noah's rainbow or something neon. Or (in a place become bilingual since Joyce left it) we may overhear something seemingly about cakes (bannocks) and not understand that 'the bannocks of Gort and Morya and Bri Head and Puddyrick, yore Loudship!' (*FW* 53.29–31) was not a recommendation of the lovely cakes of four places including Bray Head but 'the blessing' – *beannacht* – 'of God and Mary and Bridget and Patrick'. Likewise an Irish dictionary gives no help with 'mhuith peisth mhuise as fearra bheura muirre hriosmas' (*FW* 91.4–5), but if someone tells us how to pronounce these 'words' – more or less 'wit pesht wishi as fare vére mwiri hrismos' – our ears may catch 'With best wishes for a very merry Christmas'. So at the Wake we may soon feel like echoing the tongue-tied Jute: 'Boildoyle and rawhoney on me when I can beuraly forsstand a weird from sturk to finnic in such a patwhat as your rutterdamrotter' (*FW* 17.13–15). This permits the (unfounded) supposition that Baldoyle and Raheny, Dublin districts, have something to do with oil and honey, and also says that ears attuned to *beurla* (English) can understand Pat's what-is-it (patwhat, *patois*) no more than barely.

This place of traps, though, is not Eliot's 'unreal City', potent to induce spiritual malaise. As on a crisp strong sea, the dangers are bracing (a way of saying that *Finnegans Wake* is funny); and it was in his last work, even as he multiplied hazards to navigation, that Joyce at last won through to a fierce exultation in the powers of urban man that could found and elaborate such a City as the book's verbal devices imitated. 'Amtsadam, sir, to you!' (*FW* 532.6) comes the city-founder's strong voice late in the *Wake*, voicing Adam, the first man, and Amsterdam, a prototype city, and 'Amt' which is the all-purpose German word for an official functionary or his function. As an 'Amtmann' is the man in office, the magistrate, so the 'Amtsadam' would be the veritable Adam, the Founder.

'Amtsadam, sir, to you! Eternest cittas, heil! Here we are again!' (*FW* 532.6–7). This threefold utterance opens the most sustained affirmation in all of Joyce, perhaps in all modern writing: the boast of the city-founder enumerating what he has achieved. 'In pontofacts massimust' – *pontifex maximus*, in point of fact – 'I am known throughout the world wherever my good Allenglisches Angleslachsen is spoken by Sall and Will from Augustanus to Ergastulus, as this is, whether in Farnum's rath or Condra's ridge or the meadows of Dalkin or Monkish tunshep' – Rathfarnam, Drumcondra, Dalkey, Monkstown, four Dublin districts – 'by saints and sinners eyeeye alike' (*FW* 532.9–14).

'Eyeeye' is his telltale stutter, and he welters through several thousand guilt-ridden words; but his confidence is restored by the time he is calling to mind Roundwood Reservoir and the municipal water supply –

> I richmounded the rainelag in my bathtub of roundwood and conveyed it with cheers and cables, roaring mighty shouts, through my longertubes of elm: . . . I made sprouts fontaneously from Philuppe Sobriety in the coupe that's chayned for noon inebriates. (*FW* 542.4–7, 9–10)

Even the nice balance between prostitutes and police summons up his pride:

> In the humanity of my heart I sent out heyweywomen to refresh the ballwearied and then, doubling megalopolitan poleetness, my great great greatest of these charities, devaleurised the base fellows for the curtailment of their lower man. (*FW* 542.35–543.3)

For an instant the puritanic face of De Valera may be glimpsed behind the Dublin Metropolitan Police; Dev too has his place in the city's intricate story, which if it includes the bestowal of electric power – 'lamping limp from black to block, through all

Livania's volted ampire' (*FW* 549.15–16) – has more conspicuously engendered many square miles of slums where a shabby variousness challenges the statistician.

Two deadly hilarious pages are devoted to the 'respectable' slums:

> all who have received tickets, fair home overcrowded, tidy but very little furniture, respectable, whole family attends daily mass and is dead sick of bread and butter, sometime in the militia, mentally strained from reading work on German physics, shares closet with eight other dwellings, more than respectable, getting comfortable parish relief, wageearner freshly shaved from prison, highly respectable, . . . serious student is eating his last dinners, floor dangerous for unaccompanied old clergymen, thoroughly respectable, many uncut pious books in evidence, nearest watertap two hundred yards' run away, fowl and bottled gooseberry frequently on table, man has not had boots off for twelve months, infant being taught to hammer flat piano, outwardly respectable.
> (*FW* 543.21–8, 544.14–19)

– yet, compared with savagery or grunting in caves, Dublin's genteel slums too are an achievement of sorts (and they spawned Sean O'Casey), so it is precisely this long inventory of respectable poverty that *Finnegans Wake* frames with the City Charter itself, between 'This missy, my taughters, and these man, my son' and 'let them all come, they are my villeins. . . . Enwreak us wrecks' (Henricus Rex) (*FW* 543.15–16, 545.13–14, 23).

'Let them all come', let them all come indeed. The *Wake* welcomes anything congenial to quotidian experience, banal though the analytic eye may find it. 'Batch is for Baker who baxters our bread. O, what an ovenly odour! Butter butter! Bring us this days our maily bag!' (*FW* 603.7–9). Here the city is barely astir before dawn; 'It is not even yet the engine of the load with haled morries full of crates' (*FW* 604.9–11). A few early prayers are audible, but the Morris lorries are not yet abroad delivering morning milk. Elsewhere priests and servers are commencing their dialogue at early Mass –

Muta: Quodest nunc fumusiste volhvuns ex Domoyno?
Juva: It is Old Head of Kettle puffing off the top of the mornin.

Muta: He odda be thorly well ashamed of himself for smoking
before the high host.
Juva: Dies is Dorminus master and commandant illy tonobrass.
(*FW* 609.24–9)

– and a voice on the wireless is promoting a laundry:

the Annone Wishwashwhose . . . blanches bountifully and
nightsend made up, every article lathering leaving several
rinsings so as each rinse results with a dapperent roll, cuffs for
meek and chokers for sheek and a kink in the pacts for namby.
(*FW* 614.2–3, 4–7)

Out of such quotidian detail Joyce's image of the city is
assembled, splintered and enigmatic as its original. The first story
of *Dubliners* ('The Sisters', 1904) took notice of 'an unassuming
shop, registered under the vague name of *Drapery*. The drapery
consisted mainly of children's bootees and umbrellas; and on
ordinary days a notice used to hang in the window, saying:
Umbrellas Re-covered.'[15] That bland gaze at the ordinary was to
remain constant, and that calm omission to point out anything
potentially odd about the expression 'Re-covered'. The story also
records an old woman's malapropisms, *Freeman's General* (for
Journal)[16] and 'rheumatic wheels'.[17] *Finnegans Wake* (1939) still
builds on such materials, and extends such methods. It is a simple
book, really, though its simplicities so proliferate as to bewilder
the stoutest-hearted. 'My crazy tale' Joyce got around to calling
it. He'd not envisaged anything so arcane.

* * *

Engaged as we still are in understanding modernism, we need not
be surprised if sixty years ago its dynamics were not understood
at all. When *Ulysses* was published in 1922 and brought Joyce
suddenly to the notice of the world, rumours of incomprehensible
'modern art' had been abroad for some years. That was the same
year that *The Waste Land* was published, which a wag called 'the
piece that passeth understanding'. Cubist pictures had been hung
upside down. Marcel Duchamp, as everyone knew, had painted
an explosion in a shingle factory, never mind that his title said
something about a nude. Stravinsky too had been heard of, if little
heard. A bohemian conspiracy against mind was widely posited,

and whatever our subsequent sophistication we have not laid aside the old supposition that the modern movement was more unified than it in fact was. In particular we have not taken account of the comparative isolation of James Joyce, of the consistent logic by which he arrived at his procedures, of their steady evolution from one or two unobtrusively radical decisions he took very early in the course of writing some conventional-looking stories (which even then had disorienting power: publishers would accept the book, then run from it screaming).

He did not look at modern pictures, seems not to have heard modern music, read little modern literature. The avant-garde books he left behind in Paris were mostly presentation copies.

When Pound and Eliot, each on the threshold of masterly work, saluted Joyce as a master, the master they greeted had travelled by no one else's route to that rendezvous with his peers. He continued to go his own way, to their discomfiture. The best Pound could say of his last book was that a man who has made three masterworks has earned the right to experiment, and Eliot though he abetted its publication judged that one book like that was enough. Yet Joyce conformed better in his later stages than in his earlier to the aetiology of generic modernism. *Finnegans Wake*, on which he laboured for the rest of his life, is a book about a city he would never revisit, but of which he could hear the disembodied voices, after 1926, on Radio Átha Luain ('Rowdiose wodhalooing' (*FW* 324.18)), now Radio Éireann.

> missed in some parts but with lucal drizzles, the outlook for tomarry . . . beamed brider, his ability good. (*FW* 324.32–4)

It was in that book made wholly of jumbled voices that Joyce for the first time came to terms with the century's technology. It had borne his contemporaries toward new means of expression at which he had arrived by old-fashioned routes: often trivial, he conceded, 'but sometimes quadrivial'.

Notes

1 Conflated from letters of Ezra Pound to Harriet Monroe, 22 and 30 September 1914, quoted in H. Kenner, *The Invisible Poet: T.S. Eliot* (London, W.H. Allen, 1960; Methuen, 1965).
2 Virginia Woolf, *Mr Bennett and Mrs Brown* (1924), quoted in David Daiches, *Virginia Woolf* (Norfolk, Conn., New Directions, 1942), p. 144.

3 Richard Cork, *Vorticism and Abstract Art in the First Machine Age* (Berkeley and Los Angeles, University of California Press, 1976).

4 Frank Budgen, *James Joyce and the Making of 'Ulysses'* (London, Oxford University Press, 1972), p. 131.

5 Wyndham Lewis, 'Our Vortex' in *Wyndham Lewis on Art*, ed. Walter Michel and C. J. Fox (New York, Funk & Wagnalls, 1969).

6 Peter Conrad, 'A Citizen of Pandemonium', *The Times Literary Supplement*, 30 January 1976, p. 111.

7 Fritz Senn, ' "He Was Too Scrupulous Always": Joyce's "The Sisters" ', *James Joyce Quarterly*, II (1965), p. 66.

8 *Dubliners* (New York, Viking Press, 1969), pp. 153–4.

9 Ibid., p. 173.

10 Ibid., p. 172.

11 Elsewhere (H. Kenner, *Joyce's Voices* (London, Faber & Faber, 1978), ch. 2) I have named this 'the Uncle Charles Principle'.

12 All quotations are from *Collected Poems* (London, Macmillan, 1950).

13 J. M. Synge, *Works*, vol. 2 (London, Oxford University Press, 1966), p. 195.

14 *Dubliners*, p. 49.

15 Ibid., pp. 11–12.

16 Ibid., p. 16.

17 Ibid., p. 17.

James Joyce
and
his orders

Weaving, unweaving

FRITZ SENN

> Arabesquing wearily, they weave a pattern on the floor, weaving, unweaving, curtseying, twisting, simply swirling. (*U* 577)

Few works of literature, let alone novels, can have appeared more chaotic and less patterned than *Ulysses* did to its first unprepared readers. We now see it as the most multiply patterned and elaborately devised prose work ever, with the exception of *Finnegans Wake*, which, again, looks utterly chaotic but tends to be reassembled by its interpreters, that is, its discerners of patterns, as something of Viconian, ecclesiastical, cyclic, spatial, numerological, prismatic, etc., structures and orders. By 1982 we take such patterns for granted and are willing to accept yet more to be gradually uncovered. At this stage, then, equal attention might be given to the way in which all patterns are deliberately challenged. The following pages will be a detailed manifestation of what could be called The Principle of the Disrupted Pattern.

That patterns *are* disrupted is part of our surface impression of *Finnegans Wake*. Often enough we can make out ordinary language to which something seems to have happened: 'his first foetotype' (*FW* 324.1) can be seen as a thwarted attempt to say, with some redundancy, 'first prototype' with some element like 'foe' interfering. It so happens that 'prototype' means something like 'pattern' and that foes, true to type, do interfere. The reader of the *Wake* has learned to join disparate items into a new configuration: here Original Sin seems to offer itself: a first state of bliss was prototypically upset by a first adversary. But some reader might ask how 'foetus' fits into all this, which gives the whole cluster a biological tone; and again there would be a need for realignment. The same is true if we choose to read the words as a discordant spelling of 'phototype', either a technical device of printing or a metaphor, 'impression by light'. And no matter how we resystematize semantic disparity (one might, for example, link a first foe with Lucifer or Phos-phoros, the light-bearer) there seems to remain always some irritative scrap to work against interpretative complacency.

Ulysses foeto-typically opens with a quiet but memorable sentence, stately, plump, featuring a conspicuous display of shaving gear. That first close-up, 'a bowl of lather on which a mirror and a razor lay crossed' (*U* 3), will reverberate and acquire new meanings. Both bowl and mirror become transient centers of attention before long, more mirrors will turn up, as do more keen-edged cutting instruments – to say nothing of mirroring techniques or cuts and sections. The initial geometry, a cross formed on the rim of a bowl, in a novel of many symmetries and much Christian imagery, hints at spatial relationships and religious overtones, especially when the combination is solemnly 'held . . . aloft' and accompanied by an ecclesiastical, though misplaced, intonation of words from the Mass. It is difficult to imagine an extensive interpretation of the book that would *entirely* avoid recourse to bowls, vessels, mirrors, optics, circularity, crosses, crossings and all further ramifications.

Then it is all the more odd that hardly a critic feels tempted to focus on 'lather' – equally conspicuous in the opening volley – for similar symbolic or structural applications. One might, conceivably, use lather as a pivotal point for some frothy reading of the book. That does not seem to have happened yet. Somehow lather does not have quite the same appeal, and then of course *Ulysses* provides relatively scant reinforcement of the theme.

When we discover or observe some significant order in, or extract it from, or impose it on, any slice of reality or fiction, we concentrate on some elements more than others. Crossed razors and mirrors seem to function better than lather, unless someone proves otherwise. Two crossed objects on a circle form a pattern, pleasing in itself, demonstrably 'workable', in many ways: it is mirrored or varied in, say, the two crossed keys in an advertisement, the crossing paths of two keyless citizens, papal insignia, a multitude of crossings and circularities, and further trivia like crosstrees, crucified shirts, croziers, cruxes and all the rest. That first sentence, from 'Stately' to 'crossed', may verbally echo and generally prefigure the 'Stations of the Cross'. Such a clue might send some of us on a quest to excavate the neat, traditional patterns of the fourteen stations; but, though some stations are clearly mentioned, the quest would probably be a futile one; yet to overlook them completely would also misrepresent the book. Joyce later described a chapter of *Finnegans Wake* as 'written in the form of a via crucis' (*Letters*, I. 214), and *Wake* readers have been busy, and partially successful, implementing the claim. As it turns out, this takes quite a bit of machination and some pushing and stretching besides.

A circle and a cross: the possibilities are great, the vistas attractive, many results convincing and enriching. Even so we may wonder just how *does* one form a razor and a mirror into a cross on a bowl – especially the mirror – and furthermore carry the precarious arrangement, with histrionic gestures, up a steep winding staircase, then from a stairhead over to a gunrest. That takes a bit of skill too. It also enlists the cooperative game-spirit of the reader.

Even more so on the second page when we learn that there is also a brush to dip into the lather. This brush was not mentioned before, and Joyce is not a writer to forget such trifles. Mulligan presumably carried the brush in a pocket of his yellow dressing-gown since his hands were occupied 'bearing' the bowl. We guess that it was not stuck into the bowl either – something which Leopold Bloom, with practical experience, might recommend (see *U* 674). Such a protruding tool would be out of place, upsetting the initial symmetry, though a brush may fit perfectly well into some other pattern, at some other time. We may recall an earlier novel in which two brushes, of all things, suggested incipient traces of some systematic orders in an otherwise queer environment: 'The brush with the maroon velvet back was for Michael Davitt and the brush with the green velvet back was for Parnell' (*P* 7). All a matter of context, selection, arrangement.

On the whole we follow Joyce's lead when we look for patterns; like him we are purposefully, unlike him we may be unthinkingly, selective, highlighting bowls and mirrors, neglecting brushes or lather. We also force things when it helps, getting a circle from a bowl by implication or a cross from 'crossed' by back-formation, meanwhile brushing aside other potential implications not considered expedient. Stephen Dedalus uses the same tactics when displaying his literary theory. He picks suitable biographical fragments and scholarly opinions for his case but is not above some sleight of hand and a few Procrustean touches. No theorist can have patterned systems without judicious emphases and without ignoring a certain part of the evidence, and especially not without a good deal of secondary elaboration and circumstantiality. *Ulysses* is also new in integrating *this* platitude and forestalling our critical efforts about it. Patterns abound; no single one fits completely.

Being human, we want to make the randomness of experience conform to something tractable or even unifying. This is true of the Citizen in the 'Cyclops' chapter who has a formula (no matter how inconsistent) for the Irish, the British, the Jews and the foreigners; or of Bantam Lyons who tends to relate chance utterances to horse-racing; of Stephen Dedalus or Gerty Mac-Dowell or any reader of *Ulysses* who believes in Mythology, *Caritas*, Psychoanalysis, Structuralism, Connubial Amendment, Styles, or Weaving and Unweaving.

As commentators we show and analyze underlying patterns of the text. It is also part of our job to recognize that such patterns are limited, and that there are many of them, sometimes at variance with each other, and that none of them is wholly reliable or reliably whole.

A chapter like 'Wandering Rocks', for instance, lies somewhere near the center of *Ulysses*: the first chapter of the second half, according to one perspective, or the last chapter of the novel's quasi-realistic setting, or perhaps something else in yet another worthwhile system. This chapter, as the only one, is dissected into mini-episodes. This fragmentation, the synoptic tendency and the various interlacings give it the natural status of a small-scale model of *Ulysses* itself. Such an epitome is compelling and indirectly verifiable, just as we can discredit it by simple counting: nineteen sections against eighteen chapters. Close similarity, but not identity. A correlation is strongly suggested and then, irritatingly, disrupted, unless of course we clip off a section and treat it separately – the last one, for choice, as a 'coda' and in itself a recapitulation of much within the preceding eighteen parts. Or else we isolate Bloom's section, the central one.

Attempts like that have been made, will be made again, in fact should be made. The special, structural or synecdochal relation of 'Wandering Rocks' cannot easily be rejected, nor harmoniously proved without a good amount of craftiness – something of course that Odysseus was good at. Although cautious in detecting inconsistencies, he could, at a pinch, build plausible cases around a few facts.

At times it is more rewarding to stress the harmony of emergent patterns and their satisfactory coherence (Stuart Gilbert's multi-schematic inventory is the best-known example); at other times we also need a reminder of basic nonconformities. Since by now the relevance of many recognized patterns has been established abundantly, the following examples will stress what seem to be functional discrepancies – particularly in passages that appear to be most pointedly schematic.

'Several schemes' (*U* 719)

As Joyce frequently pointed out to correspondents, he had some groundplan for *Ulysses*. The so-called schemata which have been passed around show him planning and devising, and also changing his plans. Although the schemata seem to have preceded and shaped some of the writing, they also, in part, grew out of it. At any rate, we now have two authorial accounts of *Ulysses*, usually termed the Linati and the Gilbert schemata, overlapping in many details, differing in others. Whether the earlier chart, mapped out in September 1920 for Linati, remains substructurally valid or contains possibilities Joyce later rejected is a matter of debate; attempts to verify each single pristine item tend to become somewhat abstruse. The second, semi-official schema has proved useful, at least for orientation and reference. We generally find that some entries make immediate sense: kidney, tumescence, music, flesh, catechism, etc. Others are more difficult to accommodate as functionally revealing. We still don't know what 'incubism' really has to do with the 'technic' of the 'Hades' chapter. In such cases we fall back on secondary elaboration: we will find some *tertium quid pro quo*, some circuitous link, often remote. The willingness to engage in such adventurous searches and the ingenuity in their pursuits are part of the meaning which the adjective 'Joycean' has accrued. In practice most critics use at least some of Joyce's schematic pointers, often enlarging them with their own terminology. There is, seemingly, no limit to the further number of appropriate systems for a novel which complies with most and defies them all.

Beside the passages clearly hinting at some built-in ordering principles, *Ulysses* also contains less striking ones with para-schematic resonance. Premeditative Bloom, on the jakes, remembers Ponchielli's *Dance of the Hours*: 'Explain that morning hours, noon, then evening coming on, then night hours' (*U* 69). This temporal division, while not identical to Joyce's explanation to Linati, still resembles his assignment of parts of the day, along with Technics, Symbols, Organs and Colours. Bloom obliges with a colour-scheme of his own: 'Poetical idea pink, then golden, then grey, then black' (much later he even offers 'Dr Malachi Mulligan's scheme of colour', *U* 706). His attempts to justify an artefact follow close upon his vague plan to 'manage a sketch', a literary composition, by jotting down trivialities of the day, that is, amassing the sort of material that fills the book in which he is a character. In this way two paragraphs completed as early as mid-1918 already contain some hints of the method as well as a few coordinates. Bloom's time-scheme is so unassuming that it cannot be faulted, perhaps only corroborated by a corresponding one, the canonical hours dividing up the day of a priest like Father Conmee. When this scheme surfaces in 'Wandering Rocks' we learn that it can also be slightly deranged: 'Nones. Should have read that before lunch. But Lady Maxwell had come' (*U* 224).

The prospective colour-scheme too, in a novel containing twenty-one 'pinks', nineteen 'goldens' (and about a hundred instances of 'gold'), sixty-seven 'greys' and 129 'blacks' (according to Hanley's *Word Index*), can somehow be verified, at the price, naturally, of becoming commonplace and highly unspecific. Still, Bloom's poetical idea signals some kind of schema. But the author who lets Bloom tritely prophesy a possible design for the novel has, at this point, partly invalidated its specific order by launching the book with conspicuous yellow and gold on the first page; the next colours, grey and black, emerge long before the first pink in the third chapter (*U* 41). The Ponchiellian or Bloomian order – if order it is meant to project – has not been confirmed on closer inspection; and even Bloom's own next pink appears in a different sequence: 'Turning green and pink' (*U* 108). Orderly schemes are a slippery business.

'Systematisations attempted' (*U* 700)

The more *Ulysses* proceeds, the more it seems to be concerned with its own internal organization, to the point of including a few summaries of the action and summaries even of the book's own artistic devices. The built-in tentative schematizations of *Ulysses* will be illustrated by closer looks at three major synoptic abridgments: (1) Bloom's recall of the events of the day towards the end of 'Nausicaa'; (2) the list chanted by the Daughters of Erin at the end of the 'Messianic Scene' in 'Circe'; (3) Bloom's silent recapitulation of a long day (with biblical captions provided) towards the end of 'Ithaca'. These three retrospective arrangements help tie the book together and draw attention to the tying. They are also rival systems, different syntheses according to different rules, even while complementing each other and reminding us of selective principles and arbitrary omissions. They resemble whatever systems we choose to bring *Ulysses* into focus. We could easily expand the three approaches into sophisticated critical schools of various persuasions in terms of, say, reality and life (1), structure (2) and ritual (3).

As backward glances at different times, the synopses also vary in their completeness, becoming naturally more inclusive. They could be further classified by their degree of textual visibility. Bloom's fatigued recall (1) does not stand out at all and will have to be disengaged from its enveloping circumstances within a long paragraph. The listing of events in 'Ithaca' (3) takes up a paragraph of its own and can be readily isolated, yet that holds true of everything else in the chapter. The Circean chart (2) is paraded most clearly, with neat typographical alignment and a distinctive tag – 'pray for us' – in each line. It also holds a position at the conclusion of a long phantasmagoria, just before the transition to real events in Nighttown.

1   Recall: 'long day'

Bloom, about to leave the rocks of Sandymount strand, recollects the events of an already tiring day:

> Long day I've had. Martha, the bath, funeral, house of keys,
> museum with those goddesses, Dedalus' song. Then that
> bawler in Barney Kiernan's. Got my own back there. . . . What
> I said about his God made him wince. . . . Three cheers for
> Israel. . . . But Dignam's put the boots on it. Houses of
> mourning so depressing.   (U 380)

This is factual and concise, in temporal order, and in a manner
which is psychological, determined by the way Bloom would
think, feel and unconsciously select. Habitual events like meals
and shop visits do not register. His frustrated glimpse of Greek
goddesses made a greater impact than the completed visit to the
library, a professional routine. And he gives prime emphasis to
the most recent occurrences, his disagreeable visit to the Dignam
family and, above all, his encounter with the Citizen, which he
chalks up as a success. The voyeuristic score with Gerty, recent
enough to count as the present, needs no recalling. What will
become the action of the next chapter is still a future possibility:
'Call to the hospital to see.' This shortest of all summaries, and the
least problematic one, is also the only one to allow for what may
happen on the next day or days: 'Must call to those Scottish
widows as I promised' (U 380) prescribes a task Bloom is likely to
fulfill. Around that chore another Bloomsday could be built,
another novel written.

The Cyclopian details ('Three cheers for Israel. . . . What I said
about his God') refer back to Bloom's hasty self-defense, deftly
turned into an attack by his *ad hoc* schema of sorts for presenting
western civilization in terms of Jewish achievement: 'Men-
delssohn was a jew and Karl Marx was a jew and Mercadante and
Spinoza. And the saviour was a jew and his father was a jew. Your
God' (U 342). This particular schema, we know, is not universally
accepted by the opposition, and we also have little difficulty
recognizing its flaws. But we may see a similar process at work in
the partly Hebraic translation of Bloomsday in (3), a version
prepared for, moreover, by a similar, but amended, list of
'illustrious sons' (U 687).

Bloom's review of his day in 'Nausicaa' is also Homeric; it
acknowledges the account Odysseus gives of all his adventures at
the court of the Phaeacians (*Odyssey*, ix–xii).

2   *The Litany*

When the 'Circe' chapter was already well on its laborious way
Joyce kept adding more material. In the summer of 1921 he
notified Valery Larbaud: 'et j'ai ajouté à *Circe* une scène
messianique avec une litanie chantée en son honneur qui acquière
ces titres tirés des épisodes, c à d, des aventures' (*Letters*, I. 169).
The strange litany is recited by the Daughters of Erin, who are
based on the Daughters of Jerusalem (who in turn are addressed in
one of the Stations of the Cross):

> Kidney of Bloom, pray for us.
> Flower of the Bath, pray for us.
> Mentor of Menton, pray for us.
> Canvasser for the Freeman, pray for us.
> Charitable Mason, pray for us.
> Wandering Soap, pray for us.
> Sweets of Sin, pray for us.
> Music without Words, pray for us.
> Reprover of the Citizen, pray for us.
> Friend of all Frillies, pray for us.
> Midwife Most Merciful, pray for us.
> Potato Preservative against Plague and Pestilence,
>   pray for us.   (*U* 498–9)

That this list is 'drawn' from the Bloom episodes has been
recognized all along. It is a prime instance, often quoted, of 'Circe'
transcending merely psychological, individual, parapsycholo-
gical or other categories and reflecting on the book itself as a
patterned artefact.

   Joyce could have selected any number of items or salient points
from each chapter or used other formal matrices than the Litany of
the Blessed Virgin. But the Litany, as it stands, forms a tidy
referential system, and it works: an entry for each chapter, in the
right order, and each entry characteristic and representative.
Some terms, like Kidney, Bath or Music, could have been lifted
out of Joyce's schema itself. The system looks so watertight that
most of us matter-of-factly fill the slot open for 'Scylla and
Charybdis' with the available entry, 'Wandering Soap' – which is
really highly inappropriate as a heading for the Library chapter.
No doubt Bloom carried his cake of soap around there, but that

soap had wandered through every other episode too ever since it was bought. So some adjustment is called for.

Parallelism and similarity link this wandering soap to the 'Wandering Rocks' chapter (and chances are that most readers automatically make that connection unless they keep close track of the chapter sequence). For a moment the next chapter seems to replace the one in which Bloom appears only peripherally; in other words, we can perhaps take some license with the Library episode, which features Stephen and relegates Bloom to the background. We may remember that 'Scylla and Charybdis' and 'Wandering Rocks' were alternatives in the *Odyssey* and, in *Ulysses*, are bracketed in other ways as well – such observations may alert us to chapter relations in general but they do not explain the presence of the soap in the Library episode.

The soap, however, figured immediately before it. In a fluster about Boylan's unexpected appearance in Kildare Street, Bloom pretended to look for some object. His roll-call of the contents of his pockets, practically a pre-Ithacan inventory, concluded with a relieved 'Ah, soap there I yes' (*U* 183).[1] The rediscovery of that soap occurs just before Bloom reaches the gates of the museum, and the reader the Library chapter. So the soap may have some talismatic power for Bloom, comparable to the potato which is featured in 'Circe' and glorified in the entry of the Litany.

'Wandering Soap' also echoes 'wandering jew', Mulligan's reference to Bloom *in* the Library chapter (*U* 217). This would have made a suitable and specific line for the list. Maybe 'Wandering Soap' was preferred because of the initials, WS, which are those of the poet discussed in the library, William Shakespeare (much is made of names and initials and letters in the discussion). But once we concentrate on the initials of one entry and proclaim them significant, consistency brings us up against questions like a possible relationship between, for example, 'MMM' and 'Oxen of the Sun'. This approach would probably lead to little more than a waste of literal dexterity. The soap remains elusive and sticky.

The point is simply that *some* circuitous adjustment is necessary to validate the particularity of this chapter appellation. Some reader may quite possibly come up with a convincing link, but it will not be as direct as all the other links of the Litany. It will remain a matter of engineering and ingenuity. The one piece that fails to fit a conspicuous order becomes a challenge, a provocation of our restorative instincts. The disturbance of a perceived order calls for rectification through whatever detours or Daedalian cunning. No pattern is quite intact; there are both reassuring redundancies and disquieting oddities or puzzles. But in practice we tend to accept an erratic soap as part of a larger system so well in evidence as the Litany.

This larger system offers a tidy list of twelve signifiers (or eleven plus one odd one) for chapters 4–15. In itself, however, it turns out to be a strange mixture of deceitful homogeneity, not unlike many catalogues in 'Cyclops'. Most entries designate Bloom, but in strangely different ways: he is a Canvasser for the *Freeman* by profession and a Friend of all Frillies by proclivity. But only on Bloomsday does he become, accidentally a Mentor[2] of Menton and a Reprover of the Citizen. We don't know if he is, or ever was, a Mason, although the 'Lestrygonians' chapter offers at least a rumour to that effect. But in none of the foregoing senses 'is' Bloom a 'Midwife Most Merciful'; in 'Oxen of the Sun' Bloom may have felt merciful towards suffering mothers, and there is something midwifely in his sympathy in general. The leap to Bloom's *being*, however, is much bolder than in any other direct appellation, even if we grant that the transformations of 'Circe', where all these labels occur, can easily deal with categorical inconsistencies or a change of sex. Other entries do not even refer to what Bloom *is*, either actually or potentially, but to what he has on his person: soap, book, potato, perhaps also the *Freeman* newspaper (left behind in the Ormond Hotel). The list in part seems to carry on the inventory caused by Boylan in Kildare Street. Bloom was sent a yellow flower by Martha Clifford, but that is not, presumably, what 'Flower of the Bath' stands for. If we take the end of 'Lotus-eaters' for our clue, 'flower' (*U* 85) figuratively refers to Bloom's genitals. Perhaps *then* the first two entries could head a list of organs (Joyce's schemata include 'Organs'); but that system would break down right away. In any case the kidney in question is not Bloom's own but the one he prepared for breakfast (being a pork kidney, that also qualifies it for 'Circe'). And 'Music without Words' fits neither of the previous categories which the Litany prompts us into trying out. The list may ultimately remain as irreducible as the entirety of the heterogeneous material which goes into 'Circe'. Maybe we could

pigeonhole various elements according to metaphorical or meto-
nymical content, perhaps by comparing them to the Aeolian
headings (also of diverse origin) or rhetorical figures. In the
Litany's basic defiance of all systematic clutches it resembles
Ulysses with its assortment of diversified chapters, none of whose
striking characteristics could ever have been predicted from the
preceding ones.

What does unite the dozen lines is their guise as a perversion of
the words of the Litany as they were heard streaming forth from
the Star of the Sea Church in Sandymount (*U* 354 ff.). From the
snatches heard in 'Nausicaa', 'virgin most merciful' (*U* 354) has
moved across with an obstetric adaptation to 'Midwife Most
Merciful' − a conflation which somehow brings together the
female overtones (or 'Symbols', as Joyce called them in his
schemata), virgin, mother, whore, of three successive chapters
and turns them into a twisted praise of Bloom. References to the
Litany in *Ulysses* seem to be limited to 'Nausicaa', 'Oxen' and
'Circe'. 'Virgin/Midwife Most Merciful' most likely to have set
the pattern for the whole list.

Out of that pattern some shadowy alignments now appear,
similarities with the real Litany, semantic or, more aptly,
rhythmic ones, like 'Kidney of Bloom' for 'Mother of God';
'Flower of the Bath' for 'Tower of Ivory'; 'Mentor of Menton' for
'Mirror of Justice'; 'Canvasser for the Freeman' for 'Comfortress
of the Afflicted'; 'Wandering Soap' for, of all things, 'Mystical
Rose', and so on. Such acoustic approximations might result from
one's hearing the liturgical phrases faintly, from afar, not quite
catching the words and substituting others, here with Circean
transmutations of Bloomian adventures. In a way Mulligan's early
blasphemies and distortions prepared us for such near-equations.
The Circean chant and the Litany, at any rate, reflect on each
other; we are invited to make comparisons, to match parts and to
make sense of the matchings.

At some point our perplexity over the odd conglomerate may
shift to the original Litany itself. To the uninformed, Bloom as a
wandering soap is about as mysterious as the Virgin as a mystical
rose. *A Portrait* noted that 'protestants used to make fun of the
litany of the Blessed Virgin'. But Stephen was troubled by it too:
'How could a woman be a tower of ivory or a house of gold?' (*P*
35). Stephen solved the question on his own: 'By thinking of

things you could understand them'. Girls have hands like ivory: 'That was the meaning' (*P* 42). Although established theology would put it differently, Stephen — often like the reader — has nothing to go upon but his own associations and cross-references, and his wits. As it turns out, Stephen is on the right track: in the Song of Songs, some woman's neck 'is as a tower of ivory' (Song of Songs 7:4). That does not explain how this phrase became part of the Litany, but it points towards an analogy: the Litany consists of phrases taken from various parts of the Old and New Testaments, with some later adaptations. There are, at least, some compositional similarities.

None of the questions adumbrated here needs to be raised, yet they exist as potential disturbances. We can take the Circean chant as mnemotechnic guidance, or as pure fun and rest content that some conventional ceremony is being imitated. But, since it resembles the earlier litany (the word means 'prayer' or 'supplication'), we may also be led back to a related event and word in Homer's epic: when Odysseus 'besought' Circe 'by her knees' to send him home, the Greek verb is *ellitaneusa* (*Odyssey*, x. 481).

Perversely, just when the associative and phantasmal randomness of 'Circe' trims itself into a systematic architectural epitome of the central part of the book, we are confronted with more systematic dissonances and are dispatched to grope for new encompassing superschemata to accommodate all the disparate new eccentric leads.

3   Recapitulation

'Ithaca' is full of inventories and new ways of imposing order on old experience. From among its perspectival groupings emerges Bloom's last and most complete résumé, combined with what looks like one more fully fledged, schematic groundplan. It is not necessarily, or even probably, a verbatim transcription of Bloom's thoughts. The mode of the chapter, as usual, takes over and here substitutes its own pedantic regularity.

For convenience the fifteen items are here set off in separate lines:

> The preparation of breakfast   (burnt offering):
> intestinal congestion and premeditative defecation
>   (holy of holies):

the bath   (rite of John):
the funeral   (rite of Samuel):
the advertisement of Alexander Keyes   (Urim and
    Thummim):
the unsubstantial lunch   (rite of Melchizedek):
the visit to museum and national library   (holy
    place):
the bookhunt along Bedford row, Merchants' Arch,
    Wellington Quay   (Simchath Torah):
the music in the Ormond Hotel   (Shira Shirim):
the altercation with a truculent troglodyte in Bernard
    Kiernan's premises   (holocaust):
a blank period of time including a cardrive, a visit to
    a house of mourning, a leavetaking   (wilderness):
the eroticism produced by feminine exhibitionism   (rite
    of Onan):
the prolonged delivery of Mrs Mina Purefoy   (heave
    offering):
the visit to the disorderly house of Mrs Bella Cohen,
    82 Tyrone street, lower, and subsequent brawl
    and chance medley in Beaver street   (Armageddon):
nocturnal perambulation to and from the cabman's
    shelter, Butt Bridge   (atonement).   (U 728–9)

The recapitulation not only enumerates the main events and brings the former recall (1) up to date and Ithacasizes it; it also introduces a schema rivaling the familiar Homeric one (which is much more pervasive but is never stated or made explicit in the book). Joyce lifted the fifteen appellations from the Bible, with a strong Jewish bias and some emphasis on Leviticus, Exodus and Numbers in the Old Testament. The parenthetical labels were added to the page proofs of *Ulysses*, late in January 1922 (see the *James Joyce Archive*, vol. 27, pp. 204–5). The last item originally read '(peace offering)'; in a 'lettre de M. Joyce reçue le 30.1.22' it was changed to 'atonement' – one of the book's final modifications.

As if in farewell, Joyce put a last methodical stamp on the novel before abandoning it to its readers and fate. He added a strong Semitic reinforcement, a return to Bloom's roots and those of western civilization. The first terms of the series are anchored in Mosaic laws and practices, mainly rites and offerings. We might relate the whole system to one verse in Leviticus, with thirteen phrases sandwiched between the first and the last: 'And he shall put his hand upon the head of the *burnt offering*; and it shall be accepted for him to make *atonement* for him' (Leviticus 1: 4; my italics). Note that Moses appears on the same page of *Ulysses* in connection with light being extinguished and an enigma being hereby solved (*U* 729).

The list furthermore functions as an equivalent to the well-known epitome in the *Odyssey* (xxiii. 310–43), where Odysseus, finally reunited with Penelope, mentions all the incidents of his return, a précis of what he had told the Phaeacians in epic breadth and detail. The passage, in the views of philologists both ancient and modern, is considered doubtful, perhaps a later interpolation, because of some irregularities. Odysseus speaks about himself in the third person. What has given most pause is the inconsistency that the former choice between the Wandering Rocks ('*Planktas petras*') and Scylla and Charybdis now has become serial adventures: 'and had come to the Wandering Rocks, and to dread Charybdis, and to Skylla' (xxiii. 327). So that Homer too, at least in the texts as handed down to us, offers both neat confirmation of the preceding narrative and some discordant features. Joyce seems to follow suit. In fact, by giving Wandering Rocks full episodic treatment as well, he seems to have used the questionable account of Odysseus himself rather than the tale of the whole epic. And he seems to translate the Homeric epitome back to its origin according to Victor Bérard, who claimed that the *Odyssey* was a Hellenized version of the nautic lore of the Phoenicians, and so Joyce gave it a Semitic imprint, borrowing his terms from the Old Testament.

'Ecclesiastical rites' (*U* 688)

Naming is a powerful and unsettling activity; any scheme as detailed as the fifteen parenthetical headings casts some light on the episodes and raises new expectations. But, again, not all entries make immediate sense. 'Burnt offering' looks like the kidney Bloom scorched in the frying pan, forgotten there but certainly not offered. With some good will, we can relate 'the bath' to baptismal immersion by John the Baptist, etc. 'Rite of Onan' fits 'Nausicaa' up to a point (Onan was not guilty of masturbation). We will complacently find some reference to death in the Book of Samuel; we can strain 'holocaust' to cover an exaggerated account of the havoc wrought by an inefficiently hurled biscuit tin or the Citizen's maledictions, even though nothing is literally 'burned' in 'Cyclops', except perhaps the tip of Bloom's cigar. 'Holocaust' appears in the Catholic Douay version of the Bible where the King James version has 'burnt offering', which does not make for clarity or for systematic neatness – or should one therefore find a link between 'Calypso' and 'Cyclops'? Each source for our information – reference books, a Jewish encyclopaedia, Catholic or Protestant Bibles – shifts our basis of subsumption.

While 'Shira Shirim' translates into Song of Songs and so roughly fits 'Sirens', it is not at all obvious why 'Simchath Torah' ('rejoicing of the Law') should stand for 'Wandering Rocks'. A good deal of manipulation is necessary to show the relevance. Most of the Ithacan phrases are much harder to tie to their respective episodes than those in the Circean Litany. The bits of errant Jewishness challenge us, and with the ritual goals so clear in view we will of course come up with some connections. The accumulated interpretations to date, however, have not been signally successful, nor even very plausible. Such handbooks as Weldon Thornton's *Allusions in Ulysses* or Gifford and Seidman's *Notes on Joyce* atypically remain very halfhearted in trying to relate rites and offerings to the themes in the book.

'Urim and Thummim' (corrected), seemingly the most specific and precise entry, turns out to be the most elusive. Reference books and commentaries agree on just one thing: we don't know the etymology, the meaning or the import of these two terms for something worn on the breastplate of priests (Exodus 28:30). An interpreter has a conveniently wide choice of unlikely possibilities to align this entry with an advertisement of two crossed keys. It appeared in 'Aeolus', the first chapter to present a wholly new set of complications and Mosaic overtones, but we are yet waiting for a prophet to reveal what 'Urim and Thummim' cogently have to do with the chapter or the advertisement.

In her extensive study of the Bible in Joyce's works, Virginia Moseley tackles 'Aeolus' squarely and adduces a great many other

quotations, but without ever establishing any special significance, or even attempting to do so, for that 'inward illumination
symbol of the high priest's office' among the chapter's numerous
cross-references.[3] We gain little insight from 'Perhaps the Urim
and Thummim point not only to the *double entendre* of Stephen's
parable but to that of the whole episode, for that matter the entire
novel.'[4] It is clearly not that Moseley hasn't done her homework
but rather that all our collective homework – barring inspiration –
might never come up with anything more compelling. The least of
the Homeric correspondences has much more solid foundation
than this.

Almost inevitably, a detailed study of Jewish elements by
Ralph R. Joly[5] will lean heavily on those ritual terms in 'Ithaca'
and use those entries as its own chapter headings and focuses.
Joly maintains that the 'epithets' extracted out of the Jewish
ritual 'underscore the theme of *Ulysses* as ultimately an affirmation of Creation's holiness . . . and, more, specifically, that they
provide substantial hints as to the nature of Bloom's plight, the
course he must pursue, and the results readers may expect'.[6] This
is a large order. Hints are provided, surely (if hints can ever be
substantial). Ultimate affirmation is more doubtful, its acceptance
hinging on our basic attitudes, which determine what we select
out of the puzzling totality. Perhaps we should take the Mosaic-
Christian scheme straight and swallow it whole, in which case it
becomes all the more important to understand it clearly. About
'Urim and Thummim' in connection with 'Aeolus', however, Joly
has little more to offer than the vaguest speculation and perhaps
the fact that there are *two* names in the term and *two* keys, *two* key
persons in the chapter[7] – nothing stunningly substantial. Joly's
study is full of useful hints and tenuous possibilities. But there
still have to be omissions (Joly's array of chapter discussion leaves
no place for 'wilderness') as well as additions (for the chapters not
encompassed by the ritual). And, again, no convincing reason is
given for the assignment of 'Simchath Torah' for 'Wandering
Rocks' – the hints are not substantiated.

Critics like Joly, who opt for 'ultimate affirmation', tend to
approach a prominent schema within the text with no undue
levity. Their ritual solemnity would be more justified if we had
any evidence that Joyce planned the episodes with Levitical
correspondences or similar analogies in mind. He quite possibly

did, except that the valedictory additions of January 1922 look like afterthoughts, a last lick of extensional paint, and not an elaborate groundplan. In some respects they resemble the subtitles in 'Aeolus', also added in a late revision. These redirect our attention, focus on themes one might otherwise neglect, but they do not fundamentally impose overall meanings. They rather point to the questionable being of all such titles, labels or perspectives. Part of their function is in the arbitrariness they reveal.

We still need more enlightenment for the biblical labels. In the meantime there is no reason to overlook the more amusing aspects – the whole as a series of deflections, translations in the manner of Mulligan. A kidney abandoned in the frying pan may be a 'burnt offering'; a place as private and intimate as an outhouse must have been called 'holy of holies' in countless flat jokes. From such a list of banal witticisms a full system may have arisen, swathed in Ithacan puntiliousness, none of which detracts at all from its potential liturgical import. We can imagine Bloom trying out such correspondences in his mind, some process akin to his hindsight rendering of Martha Clifford's letter into some language of flowers. That earlier instance of word-association could be typographically adapted to the manner of the Ithacan catalogue, something like: 'Angry (tulips) with you darling (manflower) punish your (cactus) if you don't please poor (forgetmenot) how I long (violets) to dear (roses) when we soon (anemone) meet all naughty (nightstalk)' (U 78, parentheses added). Such a commentary could be raised, in the nights-talk of the penultimate chapter, to a ponderous floral system, with deadpan extrapolations, but we would be misleading ourselves if we treated it as nothing else.

'Chance medley' (U 729)

'Ithaca' (like 'Circe', notably) tends to treat heterogeneous material in its own idiosyncratic way, disdaining to keep deed from wish, fact from rumour, knowledge from conjecture or phantasy. The recapitulatory directions may, in Joly's words, 'form with the Homeric dimension, an important means to episode cohesion',[8] but the edifice they indicate could also be, as one of the phrases proclaims, a 'disorderly house' (*U* 729). There is both cohesion and 'chance medley' (*U* 729) – an accidental jumble of facile tags, nominal fun and occult profundities not wholly unlike the contents of the first and second drawer. Cohesion may yet be demonstrated, but until then the superimposition of what has all the trappings of the most methodical network of rites and names and offerings within the whole book produces, not radiant clarity – to say nothing of integrity and consonance – but even more loose threads for new texturings.

Such threads may lead us to more portals of discovery. 'Atonement', not loose in this way, ties 'Ithaca', the conclusion of male activities in *Ulysses*, back to 'Telemachus', where Haines mentioned a theory, a theological interpretation of *Hamlet*, 'The Son striving to be atoned with the Father' (*U* 18). 'Atoned/atonement', potent in their reverberations, appear nowhere else in the whole novel. Many interpretations have been built around them, starting with Stuart Gilbert and echoing down many critical passages. Joyce's parting shot, a few days before *Ulysses* was released, clearly stresses atonement – but atonement of whom and with whom? Outside of the schema it is not easy to locate conclusively, nor do we know if the word in its final place may not express one more of Bloom's yearnings. If we look at what happens in 'Eumaeus' and in 'Ithaca' (the recapitulation may cover both episodes) without bias it will hardly strike us that Bloom and Stephen are 'at one', literally or figuratively. Communion, or even basic communication, has to be discerned in some remoter, 'symbolic' conjunction. We do find hints to that effect, but also some against it. Nor does the future promise any togetherness either; the outcome may be that both men are able to go their own separate ways. Furthermore, only Bloom ('the Father') ever does any 'striving'; Stephen ('the Son' in Haines's words) not at all. All of which is not to say that atonement could not be constructed out of stimuli in *Ulysses*. It will be done all the more readily since the very notion of atonement is close to one of the most traditional, deepest-rooted aims of literary criticism, the unveiling of some basic oneness, some underlying unity.

The attachment of '(atonement)' to 'Butt Bridge' is curious too. Bridges of course unite (unless, for Stephen, their piers are somehow connected with Pyrrhus, a losing victor against Rome, *U* 24–5), yet the name Butt (from Isaac Butt) in Irish history conjures up thoughts, not of a happy union, but mainly of a split in the party and the usurpation of Butt's power by Parnell[9] – not that *this* is any more conclusive than Dantean imagery or 'Epps's massproduct' (*U* 677) or whatever we select for our palliative theses; it merely points out unavoidable contradictions in the choices.

Atonement takes place at some non-realistic and not immediately apparent level. Such levels are always strongly suggested, especially with the interweaving of biblical phrases. In a more pointed manner Joyce also worked in the 113th Psalm, with attendant ceremony and resumed 'intonation' (*U* 698). It is one of the best-attested facts in all *Ulysses* criticism that this particular psalm was used by Dante to decree how many senses exist in such scriptural passages. This, in turn, has led some Joyceans to specify how many levels they allow for *Ulysses*. We need only concur that, in the Bible, in Dante or in Joyce, more happens than is visible on the surface and that many systems and contexts are possible, and we are reminded that sacred scriptures were in need of interpretation long before literary texts.

One case in point, from the recapitulation, may be 'Shira Shirim', the Song of Songs or Solomon's Canticle of Canticles. With its sensual appeal and beauty of language, this book, on its surface, is a love or wedding song. Whatever else it is is subject to much argument and speculation: its sexuality, above all, had to be allegorized. The most daring interpretation is the one put forth by the Catholic Church which sees in it 'the happy union of Christ and his Spouse . . . the Church'. So the Church itself interprets itself into the song (a common occurrence of *all* interpretation), and thereby as endearing and memorable a verse as 'Thy two breasts are like two young roes that are twins, which feed among the lilies' (Song of Songs 4:5) is 'to be understood as the love of God and the love of our neighbour . . . which feeds on the divine mysteries and the holy sacraments'.[10] Solomon himself would hardly have agreed, and the Christian reading of the passage is clearly retrospective. Joyce himself must have been exposed, when young, to many such analogies so that, for this reason alone, they would pass into his works. The point here is, again, that, to the uninitiated, such daring translations *appear* farfetched or forced. In labeling the events in the Ormond Hotel 'Shira Shirim' Joyce also acknowledges an allegorical tradition and parodies it.

We are at least invited to consider *two* rival interpretations of the Song of Songs – a Judaic reading or a later Catholic one, one according to Bloom's forgotten roots or to Stephen's disowned fixations. Joly concentrates on Jewish elements, Moseley on the Bible as understood by Protestant theology. And we note in passing that scriptural interpretations at times resemble the more tenuous exercises of Joyceans in search of affirmative reductions.

In his treatment of 'Sirens' Joly claims that 'Shira Shirim' 'is Joyce's clue to the structural base for the episode's action'. Via a hypothesis (one among many possible others), that the Song of Songs is 'a story of a maiden's fidelity to her own lover despite the wooing of a king', he marshals some tenable but not overly stringent links and no lucid substantiation. The Song of Songs provides 'a hint of the outcome of the novel: that it will end in reconciliation'.[11] This is quite within the range of Ulyssean possibilities; it just does not seem to arise, very specifically, from 'Shira Shirim'. In her approach Moseley has several pages of inventive tangles, from all parts of the Bible and many parts of *Ulysses*, without making it clear why Solomon's Song should have more bearing on 'Sirens' than any other book, such as Proverbs. Practically any part of any sacred scripture would yield the same message, for it is the purpose of religious texts to hold out conditional promise for reconciliation or salvation. That the Song of Songs is really a 'firm structural base' – which of course occurrence within an accentuated schematic context prompts us to assume – remains to be proven.[12] If proof arises, chances are that new dissonances and more schematic irregularities may be entailed.

'Synopsis of things in general' (*U* 644)

The three extended synopses stimulate many more comparisons than could even be sketched here. They present different points of view. Only the Litany (2) is organized according to chapter divisions, one of the most pronounced characteristics of *Ulysses*. By contrast, recalls (1) and (3) both specify events that the novel neglects to treat in detail: the two hours between Barney Kiernan's premises and Sandymount strand, when Bloom was taken to the house of the Dignam family. This interlude, as the two reminiscences indicate, *could* have become another episode but didn't. So we have a biblical heading ('wilderness') for a nonexistent section, one 'lodged in the room of infinite possibilities' and 'ousted' by the author (see *U* 25). Yet this is in keeping with 'Ithaca', suggesting the novel's untapped possibilities. We are also given new information; it is only now that we learn that Bloom also walked through Bedford Row.

The synopses mainly corroborate each other and overlap with the kind of parallactic disparity that the novel leads us to expect. All three accounts, for example, mention the Citizen, with some variation: 'that bawler', 'the Citizen', 'a truculent troglodyte'. The last reference departs slightly from Ithacan stylistics: in strict terminology, the one the chapter affects, he is not a 'cave-dweller'; 'troglodyte' inconsistently squints at Homer's Polyphemus. The highest degree of concordance comes from the threefold repetition of the lotophagian 'bath/Bath' – but there was no bath in the chapter's events except as an anticipatory vision, so the common denominator is something external to the action in 'Lotus-eaters', and the unique schematic agreement appears a trifle askew.

Then there are notable divergences. Bloom's first recall did not register any event for 'Calypso', while his recapitulation has two headings for it (and three separate items: breakfast, congestion and defecation). Conversely Bloom initially gave 'Lotus-eaters' more extended treatment, Martha *and* the bath. In its self-reflections, *Ulysses* both confirms the divisions it imposes on its material and suggests alternative divisibilities.

Among our concerns about the validity of systems, we may also note that some major themes never even end up in any of the three nets flung at the novel. The last-minute recapitulation with its pointedly Jewish perspectives strangely ignores most of the other important Old Testament themes, such as 'house of bondage', Pisgah sight or Elijah. The synopses further omit any reference to Stephen Dedalus and his impact on Bloom, or perhaps only secondarily include him through 'atonement'. Many minor events go unrecorded, for example the consequential encounter with Bantam Lyons. But, most significantly, we would never suspect from the three lists that there is such a person as Hugh Boylan: he was, after all, seen three times and thereby deflected Bloom twice from his course, and he remains omnisuppressed in Bloom's mind throughout. So perhaps as extended summaries the synopses amount to an elaborate device to ignore Boylan.

There will always be things left out – as Molly Bloom, the arch-unweaver of webs in *Ulysses*, brings out by reiterated mistake: 'asking me had I frequent omissions where do these old fellows get all the words they have omissions' (*U* 770) – and there will always be mysteries, as the three 'enigmas', immediately following Bloom's recapitulation, testify, some 'comprehended', some not (*U* 729). The enigmas give way to yet another partial account of the day in terms, not of achievement, but of 'imperfections' and 'failure'. We also know that Bloom's ultimate recall, the chronicle of events as told in compliance with 'catechetical interrogation', is strategically doctored, modified by omissions and fictional additions, but also by the truthful mention of occurrences which Bloom wants to have singled out (*U* 735). Bloom's own depiction of Bloomsday is offstage, presented obliquely, by absence and deviations, as though we could posit some unquestionable narrative usage so obvious that, on the basis of a few particularities and exceptions, the reader could bypass the actual tale. When in fact we have had the hardest of times, all along a jerky progress, to adapt to all the narrative whims and divergences and to learn that the thing told is not ever to be extricated from the telling itself. Which reader would not be curious to know, given the reciprocal awkwardness of a couple reunited in a second-best, used bed where the husband's memoirs of his day function to leave *hers* unmentioned, what exactly it was that Bloom said? Judging from her later recollection, he seems to have been strong on chance encounters with Hynes and Josie Powell Breen and, on occasion, to have risen to his role of someone casually remembering trivia: 'who did I meet ah yes I met do you remember Menton and who else who let me see' (*U* 739).

'Unaltered by modifications?' (*U* 735)

Perhaps the most poignantly paradoxical single word of all the Ithacan refractions is the curt answer to the question 'Was the narration otherwise unaltered by modifications?', the answer being 'Absolutely' (*U* 735), one of the strongest possible terms. Bloom might have said that (even if it does not sound like him) if he were ever questioned, a mere, blunted intensive affirmation. But if we imagine how anything Bloom, even with the best intentions, might tell *could* be 'absolutely unaltered', if we try to imagine how that could be true of any narration ever, especially when the book at hand shows that all narration *is* modification, that *Ulysses* is a series of textual variants (and when, to confirm this, the tabulation on the same page lists the veracious mention of *Sweets of Sin* AS a modification), then we realize that 'Absolutely' means something like a vague 'more or less; to the best of his ability' or that, more precisely, it means *relatively*.

Once more, by the way, Homer has preceded *Ulysses*. When Odysseus, repeatedly covering his true identity by cunning stories about his origin and voyage, is finally recognized by Penelope and retails his real adventures in the epitome of Book XXIII, he does so with no strident falsehoods, but not absolutely without modifications either. The inclusion of Wandering Rocks as an actual hazard is a minor itinerary detail which would hardly matter much to his wife at this juncture. But Odysseus gives no inkling of the princess Nausikaa: 'Next how with great toil he came to the Phaeacians, who gave him all worship heartily, as to a god, and sent him with a ship to his own dear country'. Yet Circe and Calypso, with whom the better part of the ten years were spent, could not be omitted. Odysseus reports correctly, but does not go out of his way to rub in any involvement of his own: 'Then he told all the wiles and many contrivances of Circe'. And we would never guess that, at least for a while, the nymph on Ogygia had been pleasing him: 'And how he came to the isle of Ogygia, and to the nymph Calypso, who kept him there in her hollow caves, longing to have him for lord, and nurtured him and said that she would make him never to know death or age all his days'.[13] Such a factual but not all-inclusive account is what one would expect of a returning husband. We do not know how wise Penelope took it all. She, and her husband, fell asleep.

Molly Bloom, however, stays awake, troubled and ruminating, but with reservations about his tale: 'if it was down there he was really and the hotel story he made up a pack of lies to hide it planning' (*U* 739). She speculates on what may have happened and imposes more interpretations, and her own reminiscences contain a new set of loose threads in need of continued weavings.

Ulysses is closer to *Finnegans Wake* in its modifying tactics than the comparatively non-infringed language seems to indicate. It is our reading experience and our increasing alertness which tell us that 'Absolutely' means something else. In this respect *Finnegans Wake* is, ironically, less devious; it forgoes the pretense of such claims and tends to dangle dubious variants, with partly discoverable interferences, in front of us, like 'Obsolutely', 'aspolootly', 'Hopsoloosely' or even 'alpsulumply' (*FW* 90.20, 372.34, 413.27, 595.19), as though to scream from the housetops that obsoletion, loot or lumpishness counteract the very notion of absoluteness. It ought to be pointedly the term that is free of appearance and probability: 'amsolookly' (*FW* 404.32). It is difficult even to imagine anything absolute, something 'loosened' entirely, in the *Wake*, so it naturally disintegrates into fleeting states like 'hapsalap . . . hipsalewd . . . hopesalot . . . hoopsaloop' (*FW* 325.7).

Finnegans Wake relativates throughout; it also modifies and recapitulates, recalls and recoils. And it rephrases our reading odysseys repeatedly, perhaps most aptly in 'It is a sot of a swigswag' (*FW* 597.21) – a swigswag, among other things, from primeval chaos to provisional order, to improved order, to readjustment to comprehensive coordination, to fresh unsettling departures . . . 'systomy, dystomy'. In the rhythms of our heartbeat, systematic contractions and patternings are followed by cuttings apart (*dys, tome*),[14] or by some evil speech (*dy-stomein*, to speak evil), which is often nonconforming. Every pattern-shaping cohesive *sys-* (or original *syn-*), prefixed and between, is succeeded by a disruptive *dys-* in a Wakean or Ulyssean ecology.

* * *

Every now and then it is time for a new dystomous signal, when so many systomatic schemas are sufficiently acknowledged. This unsystematic probe into specific details and planted irritants aims to cross-reference the obvious plurality of our systematizations. To trust, overly, in any one of them is not without hazards. We might need, on occasion, more awareness of our own Procrustean techniques, never quite adequate for all the Protean resilience of the works and all their kaleidoskeptic turns.

Notes

1 This is the emended reading as proposed by Hans Walter Gabler in his booklet: *James Joyce Ulysses II.5,* prototype of a critical edition in progress,

prepared with the help of Michael Groden, Danis Rose, Charity Scott Stokes and Wolfhard Steppe (Munich, 1979). The Rosenbach version had 'Ah soap there I yes.'

2 Menton specifically belongs to 'Hades', but 'Mentor', Homerically, would be a disturbance. Mentor is the name of an Ithacan friend of Odysseus but, more prominently, a favourite shape which Pallas Athene assumes. They only appear in the *Telemachiad* and again in the *Nostos*. So the one overtly Homeric pointer in the whole catalogue is out of place.

3 Virginia Moseley, *Joyce and the Bible* (De Kalb, Illinois, Northern Illinois University Press, 1967), pp. 82–3.

4 Ibid., pp. 87–8.

5 Ralph Robert Joly, 'The Jewish Element in James Joyce's Ulysses', dissertation (University of North Carolina at Chapel Hill, 1973; University Microfilms, Ann Arbor, Michigan).

6 Ibid., Summary (unpaginated).

7 Ibid., pp. 132–4.

8 Ibid., p. 3.

9 'Parnell ousted Isaac Butt from leadership' is Joyce's own gloss (*Letters*, I. 248, 15 November 1926) on 'a kidscad buttended a bland old isaac' (*FW* 3.11), in which phrase the tricking of blind father Isaac about Esau's birthright does also not suggest happy atoned filial or fraternal relations but a progression of conflicts.

10 Introductory note to Solomon's Canticle of Canticles, and footnote to 4:5, *The Holy Bible* (Douay, 1609; Rheims, 1582), Published as Revised and Annotated by Authority (London, Burns and Oates, 1914), pp. 865 and 867.

11 Joly, op. cit., pp. 215, 216.

12 One might even make a virtue out of perplexity. What qualifies 'Shira Shirim' for 'Sirens' (beyond the meaning 'song') might be the very fact that pure interpretations needed to refine the sensuality of the song mystically out of awareness. In similar intent Bloom *tries* to forget any thought of the imminent carnality in his own house and concentrates on any distraction available, notably the songs coming from the next room.

13 *Odyssey* (xxiii. 338–40, 321, 333–6), in the translation of Butcher and Lang which Joyce knew. The translators obligingly carry the expurgation a little further, substituting 'lord', in Calypso's wishes, for a much more connubial *potis* = husband. An interesting touch is that Circe's characteristics, 'wiles and many contrivances', are precisely those of Odysseus himself, as if the emphasis were put on only their cunning being matched, and nothing else.

14 The *New English Dictionary* gives 'Dystome' and 'Dystomous', 'cleaving with difficulty'.

James Joyce
and
the body

James Joyce and the body

E. L. EPSTEIN

Many writers treat the body only as a lay figure, or as an armature necessary for the construction of the soul, but not of much importance in itself. Dickens, for example, does not change Esther Summerson's irritating mixture of self-praise and mock modesty even when Esther becomes disfigured by smallpox and (temporarily) blind. Henry James does not change the personality of Milly Theale even when she is dying, nor are bodies ever considered by James as important as annual income; both matters are irrelevant for him. Even Lawrence, surely an advocate of body consciousness, achieves, on the whole, a generalized picture of dark forces in the place of literal descriptions of bodily functions, of the body's interaction with the soul. Joyce, almost alone among novelists, seems to consider it necessary to describe even the most embarrassing bodily functions as matter suitable for literature. As I hope to show, Joyce considered that the most important functions of the soul – creation and destruction – were intimately associated with the growth and decay of the body. (Throughout this paper I will be discussing the male body. Only a woman can testify to Joyce's accuracy, or lack thereof, in describing the female body.)

James Joyce describes the surfaces of the world, human and non-human. In *Dubliners*, *Portrait* and most of *Ulysses* and *Finnegans Wake*, he refrains from direct comment on the depths of the human soul. If we are to examine Joyce on the human personality, we must examine the evidence he has given us – dialogues in the books, interior monologue (the surface of the mind), hallucination in 'Circe' (interpretations of the mind's depths), the verbal conveying of dreams in the *Wake*. Joyce seems to agree with Lawrence (one of the few points of agreement) that writers who regard the unconscious and subliminal as areas easy to partition and describe are not sufficiently respectful of the mysteries of the human personality.

The task of examination is made easier for us in the case of Joyce than it would be for Lawrence. For Joyce, the individual – soul and body – is an assemblage of 'new secondhand clothes' that is gathered together for a voyage. The fundamental events in a man's life are basically the same as those in any other man's life; the fundamental events in a woman's life are basically the same as those in any other woman's life. A human life that is not cut short or otherwise aborted (morally or physically) follows the same pattern as those of the lives of other representatives of the species. This is the lesson of *Finnegans Wake*, a palimpsest which derives its complexities from the (ultimately) insignificant differences between persons and its simplicities from the (ultimately) significant similarities.

Examination of *Dubliners*, *Portrait* and *Ulysses* gives us case histories of individuals who fit into general patterns. In *Dubliners* we find the aborted results of the attempts to grow human beings in an inhospitable climate – failed fathers, ignorant swains, frozen maids, aged children, husbands who cannot succeed in being loved by their wives. In each of the stories the basic human pattern – birth, learning, maturity, love, marriage, children, aging, death – throws off its failures. What is paralyzed in the Irish city is growth. The city-giant father of Irish history has an 'eatupus complex' (*FW* 128.36), and those who trudge through his paved and trafficked bowels are resisting his digestive processes, some more successfully, some less, some not at all. A father – whether a flesh father or a stone one – derives his fatherhood from the existence of his children. If they show signs of maturity – love, sex, independence – his fatherhood is threatened; he begins the retreat to the status of grandfather. *L'art d'être grand-père* is not a fine art, and certainly not an attractive one. The *grand-père* – no matter what his title – smokes his tobacco in the woodshed or mumbles his snuff in someone else's house. In *Dubliners* the city-father is all too successful in keeping his children childish: Little Chandler, Farrington (beaten by his society and passing on the beating metaphorically and actually), Maria (with the diction of a five-year-old girl and the disappointments of a long life), Eveline (frozen into immobility by her actual and her larger fathers), the boy in 'Araby', the men in 'Two Gallants', Gabriel Conroy, all taking the wrong road to romance – these are the casualties of the father's digestion.

In *Portrait* Joyce presents a character successfully resisting digestion. The father attacks Stephen three times by violence – once when young Stephen is forced to hide under the table, once when he is beaten by Father Dolan, and once when he is verbally assaulted by the hell-fire sermon. Stephen is also attacked by cunning several times – by the dean of studies and by Cranly, most notably. At the end of *Portrait* Stephen seems to be triumphant, but in *Ulysses* we see him resisting the most powerful effort of the father to reduce him to nullity.

In the early books, therefore, a pattern of development emerges. The soul either grows or is paralyzed. If it grows, it grows towards the possibility of creation, either of children or of art. The soul desires to project its image of itself outside of itself, to contemplate itself, as God does in the universe, or as Simon Dedalus, Buck Mulligan and Stephen Dedalus do in various shaving-mirrors. Therefore, we can begin to discern Joyce's view of the soul even though Joyce himself does not make it explicit. What the soul is – the form of forms – becomes clear as we examine significant incidents in *Ulysses* and *Finnegans Wake*. What it is not is also clear – it is not a Freudian, or Jungian, or Reichian organism, describable and mappable by therapists. It is the human being in substance, whatever the accidents may be. The accidents may be flesh or paper, stone or hypostatized energy; under the accidents, the substance remains.

In this paper, I shall examine parts of *Ulysses* and *Finnegans Wake* in an attempt to describe the effect of the changes of the body on the Joycean soul.

Death and art

In *Ulysses* the depths of the soul emerge only in the 'Circe' episode. In the rest of the book Joyce gives us the surface of the mind – the interior monologue, which represents the efforts of the mind to order the stream of sensation, and its own tentative interpretations of the stream, into the elements of the ego – and various stylistic devices that move us farther from the souls of

his characters and closer to his. The hallucinations in 'Circe' may
not be actual mental structures naturalistically conveyed; they
may be as much creations of the Irresponsible Narrator as the
expansions in 'Cyclops' or the parodies in 'Oxen'. Even if this is
so, the narrator is not spinning these hallucinations entirely from
his own bowels; they contain recognizable fantasies (turned into
words, to be sure) which represent elements of the depths of the
soul. It is here, or no place, that we shall find the fundamental
structures of the soul, clearly displayed.

It is with a clearly fundamental display that I shall begin.

> (*A skeleton judashand strangles the light. The green light wanes
> to mauve. The gasjet wails whistling.*)

THE GASJET
Pooah! Pfuiiiiii!

> (*Zoe runs to the chandelier and, crooking her leg, adjusts the
> mantle.*)

ZOE
Who has a fag as I'm here?

LYNCH
(*Tossing a cigarette on to the table.*) Here.

ZOE
(*Her head perched aside in mock pride.*) Is that the way to hand
the *pot* to a lady? (*She stretches up to light the cigarette over the
flame, twirling it slowly, showing the brown tufts of her armpits.
Lynch with his poker lifts boldly a side of her slip. Bare from the
garters up her flesh appears under the sapphire a nixie's green. She
puffs calmly at her cigarette.*) Can you see the beauty spot of my
behind?

LYNCH
I'm not looking.

ZOE
(*Makes sheep's eyes.*) No? You wouldn't do a less thing. Would
you suck a lemon?

> (*Squinting in mock shame she glances with sidelong meaning at
> Bloom, then twists round towards him, pulling her slip free of
> the poker. Blue fluid again flows over her flesh. Bloom stands,
> smiling desirously twirling his thumbs. Kitty Ricketts licks her
> middle finger with her spittle and* [,] *gazing in the mirror,
> smoothes both eyebrows. . . .*)   (*U* 510–11)

Zoe's backview precipitates a hallucination, the appearance of Lipoti Virag, Bloom's paternal grandfather. But this hallucination, which lasts for twelve pages on and off (*U* 511–23), is unlike any of the other twelve major hallucinations in the chapter[1] in two related respects. In all the other hallucinations, either there are precedents in the rest of the chapters of *Ulysses* for the content of the hallucination, or they are gigantic remodelings of public ceremonies (like Bloom's career as emperor president and king chairman). The Lipoti Virag episode is a personal family hallucination, but, unlike the others, there is no precedent in the other chapters for the bizarre hobgoblin that appears after Bloom has perceived Zoe's behind. Lipoti Virag's only rivals for bizarre behavior – The End of the World, and the Hobgoblin – have no 'real-life' analogues. (The End of the World derives from an overheard fragment of conversation.) Virag is so utterly extravagant, unlike anyone even hinted at in the previous text, that one may look for hidden meaning in him.

Since the major hallucinations (and most of the minor ones) are all responses to elements in the naturalistic dialogue of 'Circe',[2] it is possible to see the wild extravagance of Virag as Bloom's response to the sight of his supremest object of desire. It requires no demonstration that behinds (female) are Bloom's most desired object (and, probably, Joyce's). The sight of Zoe's bottom, the bottom of animate life,[3] produces a violent reaction inside Bloom's soul – his soul splits in two. His deepest drives, his basic energy, emerges as Virag; what is left comments languidly as Bloom, or behaves in a feebly romantic manner as Henry Flower. Virag appears so strange because he is truly the deepest part of Leopold Bloom. If depth-analysis of general male personality is ever to be found in Joyce, it is here, in the description of Noman.

To decipher what Joyce is saying about the deepest layers of the soul we must answer two questions:

1 Why is Lipoti Virag chosen for this role?
2 What is in the depth of the soul?

The answer to one question will assist in deriving the answer to the second.

The significance of Lipoti Virag

Literally, Lipoti Virag is Bloom's grandfather. He is the father of
Rudolph Bloom (Virag), and the son of a man who saw Maria
Theresa of Austria.[4] We know very little about Lipoti Virag from
sources outside *U* 511–23. He is referred to by name briefly at *U*
437, and again by name at *U* 723, where his photographed likeness
is referred to.[5] On the literal level, he is a completely minor
character in the text; why has he such a complex and crucial role?

Examination of his symbolic role in the book produces useful
information. The Homeric parallels are suggestive. The legitimate
grandfather of Odysseus, Autolycus, was a most distinguished
thief and deceiver, and if an analogue were necessary to find for
Lipoti Virag, the indecent sexologist, the pornographer who
disclosed 'the sex secrets of monks and maidens', Autolycus may
be the man. However, Autolycus was Odysseus' maternal
grandfather, not his father's father (the colorless Arcisius).

There is another line of paternal descent for Odysseus, one
which reveals an unexpected source for Lipoti's spasmodic
wildness. There was a tradition, with which Joyce was familiar,
that Odysseus' real father was the rogue and *débrouillard*
Sisyphus, who is probably the Homeric analogue for Rudolph
Bloom, the seller of doubtful merchandise.[6] Sisyphus' father,
Odysseus' putative grandfather, was Aeolus. Joyce's Aeolus,
Myles Crawford, exhibits the same unbridled behavior as Lipoti,
and also finds it difficult to refrain from ejaculating wild words:
'North Cork militia! . . . We won every time! North Cork and
Spanish officers! . . . In Ohio! . . . Ohio!' (*U* 127). Lipoti Virag
appears again at *U* 552 in response to a reference to the cushions,
warm from Florry's bottom, where he is dressed in a costume
extravagantly derived from Myles Crawford's appearance: '(*A
birdchief bluestreaked and feathered in war panoply*)' (see also *U*
458). Myles Crawford is a lord of (journalistic) language and has
difficulty in controlling his own linguistic flow, as has Lipoti.[7]

Lipoti Virag is a lord of language, therefore. In fact, he may be
the *source* of language – syntax and semantics. Words pop out of
him almost without motivation:

In a word, Hippogriff.   (*U* 512)

Parallax! . . . Pollysyllabax!   (*U* 512)

Tumble her. Columble her. Chameleon. (*U* 512)

Lyum! . . . Lycopodium. . . . Slapbang! There he goes again.
(*U* 513)

Huguenot. . . . It is a funny sound. (*U* 514)

Pomegranate! . . . Keekeereekee! (*U* 515)

Pretty Poll! . . . Nightbird nightsun nighttown. Chase me,
Charley! Buzz! (*U* 515)

Bubbly jock! Bubbly jock! (*U* 516)

Flipperty Jippert. (*U* 519)

Piffpaff! Popo! . . . Pchp! . . . Prrrrrht! (*U* 520)

Apocalypse. (*U* 520)

Dreck! (*U* 522)

Quack! (*U* 523)

He almost might be the young boy in 'The Sisters', pondering over the sound of *gnomon, simony, paralysis*. Here we have a linking of the most basic, most violent forces of the soul and the forces of language. The Id and the Parole have the same source.

Syntax also has its source in Lipoti. Virag attempts to say, 'Cows with distended udders have been known' to seek out serpents for relief of their overburdened udders (Bloom finishes the sentence for him), but paradigms of syntax cling to Lipoti's emerging sentence; relative, personal and demonstrative pronouns and definite articles stud the emerging syntagma: 'that the cows with their those distended udders that they have been the known' (*U* 516). No wonder Bloom feels like screaming; basic functional linguistic structures have torn loose and are floating to the surface.

Since Lipoti is the source of language, both diction and syntax, one would expect that the rest of Bloom, what is left of him after Lipoti has been subtracted, would be as linguistically boneless as it is feeble in personality (after the instinctual drives are subtracted, what remains but languor?). Bloom makes only gentle, regretful comments, in a boneless, melting, finally structureless syntax:

BLOOM

Rosemary also did I understand you to say or willpower over
parasitic tissues. Then nay no I have an inkling. The touch of a
deadhand cures. Mnemo?   (*U* 514)

BLOOM

I wanted then to have now concluded. Nightdress was never.
Hence this. But tomorrow is a new day will be. Past was is
today. What now is will then tomorrow as now was to be past
yester. . . .

BLOOM

Bee or bluebottle too other day butting shadow on wall dazed
self then me wandered dazed down shirt good job I . . . (*U* 515)

BLOOM

(*Absently.*) Ocularly woman's bivalve case is worse. Always
open sesame. The cloven sex. Why they fear vermin, creeping
things. Yet Eve and the serpent contradict. Not a historical fact.
Obvious analogy to my idea. Serpents too are gluttons for
woman's milk. Wind their way through miles of omnivorous
forest to sucksucculent her breast dry. Like those bubbly-
jocular Roman matrons one reads of in Elephantuliasis.

(*U* 516)

Henry Flower, who takes over from 'Bloom' as the other parts of
the personality, can contribute only a few lines from love-songs of
a gentle, melancholy cast, while Virag is flying into an epileptic
fury of vituperation and sexual automatism: '(*With gibbering
baboon's cries he jerks his hips in the cynical spasm.*) Hik! Hek! Hak!
Hok! Huk! Kok! Kuk!' (*U* 521).

It seems clear that for Joyce rage, sexual drive and language
come from the same part of the soul, the deepest part. The 'pshent'
Lipoti wears (*U* 511) is perhaps the sign of Thoth ('god of libraries,
a birdgod, moonycrowned . . . they [books] are still. Once quick
in the brains of men. Still: but an itch of death is in them, to tell me
in my ear a maudlin tale, urge me to wreak their will' (*U* 193–4).
Lipoti is certainly a 'birdgod', specifically a secretary-bird
(*sagittarius serpentarius*), as the two quills projecting over his ears
and the roll of parchment under his arm testify. (See also *U* 552,
quoted above.) In Lipoti Virag we find the source of libraries, odd

as it may seem.[8] If he is the origin of libraries, he is also the source of *Ulysses*, the linguistic impulse as well as the source of violence and aggression. But, again, why is it Bloom's grandfather that represents the emotion-linguistic demon? Why is Lipoti Virag 'basilicogrammate', the sovereign word?

Lipoti is a grandfather, and grandfathers and greatgrandfathers in *Ulysses* are not simply the husks of former fathers; they are associated with symbols of bodily death. At *U* 114 Bloom sees a rat crushing itself under the plinth of a monument in Glasnevin. 'An old stager: greatgrandfather: he knows the ropes,' thinks Bloom. The rat is referred to again at *U* 117, *U* 273 and *U* 279. The rat and the greatgrandfather are associated in Bloom's mind. The greatgrandfather rat becomes a 'grandfather rat' on *U* 474; the rat is toddling after Paddy Dignam. It is just before the first introduction of the 'obese grey rat', the greatgrandfather rat (*U* 114), that Bloom imagines the recorded voice of greatgrandfather declaring that he is awfully glad to see you again. Out of the complex of emotional materials in *Hades* a link is forged between the symbol of beastly death, the rat, and remote ancestors. The strangeness of the past which is yet familiar, because time is cyclical, merges with the fear of bodily extinction. Stephen has his symbols of beastly death – dogs; Bloom adopts dogs in this sense, but he adds rats to the list. When Lipoti is ready to depart, he sloughs his skins and exclaims, 'Rats!' (*U* 522)

The fear of bodily death (always contrasted with the love of life, the promised land, Molly's bottom and her animal warmth (*U* 734)) pursues Bloom through the book. From 'Calypso' onward the 'cold oils' (*U* 61) of fear 'slide along his veins' at the thought of physical extinction. The association is given symbolic force in 'Cyclops'; the Polyphemus-Citizen sends the dog after Bloom[9] just as the original Polyphemus sends his father, Poseidon ('Old Father Ocean', *U* 50), after Odysseus. Polyphemus prays for death for Odysseus, and the Citizen sends Garryowen after Bloom on the same mission. Indeed, the dog hunts Bloom all through 'Circe': *U* 437 (where the 'retriever' introduces the first phantom, Rudolph Bloom), *U* 441, *U* 448, *U* 449, *U* 452, *U* 453 (where the dog is called Garryowen), *U* 454 (by this time he has become a wolfdog, a mastiff, a spaniel and a bulldog), *U* 472–4 (where the 'beagle' becomes the animated corpse of Paddy Dignam and after whom the grandfather rat toddles), *U* 502 (perhaps), *U* 520–1 (when

Lipoti Virag becomes a dog), *U* 572 (however, here the pack of staghounds is after the fox Stephen), *U* 586 (now the pack of bloodhounds is after Bloom), *U* 587, *U* 600 (Dog as the opposite of the redeeming God), *U* 601–2, and finally at *U* 609, where the fear of death barks from a distance against the defending father and the helpless son.

Fear of bodily extinction and desire for the promised land of Molly's bottom merge at the sight of Zoe's nether regions and precipitate Lipoti Virag. Joyce here suggests that the root of linguistic creativity is to be found in the depths of the soul, where side by side exist Love and Death. Eros and Thanatos lie together in the psychic bed in both Joyce and Freud.[10] In Joyce, it is literature which is produced by their union. In *Ulysses* the soul, recoiling from death of the body, urges itself strongly toward the Promised Land of Eros and in its voyage eastward scatters letters in its wake.

Life and art

In the *Wake*, the night book, the body is asleep. All action is interior. In *Ulysses*, a day-and-night book, at least half of the book is devoted to daylight hours. Daylight allows the sense of sight to perceive the novelties of the world, the Protean shift of daytime stage properties that intrigue the mind and challenge it. As the novelties crowd into the eye at a rate of a million bits of information a second, the mind attempts to make sense of the elements of flow. It restricts its conscious regard to those elements that seem most valuable to it at the moment, and therefore it fits in the concreted masses of valued experience into its memory as words. Here sight becomes sound; novelty becomes experience. The interior of the mind for Joyce is a phantasmagoria of images becoming language. In this Joycean psychological schema, Eros is represented by the embracing of novelty; in heterosexual love, desire is directed at a body which is not and can never be a solipsistic projection of your own bodily image. Eros, innocently and freely, embraces novelty. However, Thanatos fearfully presses novelty into rigid systems of experience.[11] In *Ulysses* the outdoors daytime chapters are devoted to the processing of novelty innocently gathered. It is when darkness falls that the interior of the mind attempts to wrestle innocence into experience. No wonder the style of *Ulysses* becomes capricious as the light wanes! Even during the daytime, elements of irresponsibility creep into the text when an episode is set in an interior, as in 'Scylla and Charybdis'. In this chapter, Stephen emerges from the library 'out of the vaulted cell into a shattering daylight of no thoughts' (U 215). The acceptance of shattering daylight is Eros; in Nighttown Eros is accepted by the shattering of a shade. Thoughts are Thanatos; the shattering of one form is followed by the creation of another by the soul, the form of forms. 'Penelope', the celebration of Eros, takes place as the sun is rising for a new day of no thought. Ulysses is as much a cyclical book as the Wake.

The body represents novelty for the mind: our knowledge of our own bodies is both more intimate and more oblique than our knowledge of the bodies of others, and much of our discovery of our bodies is necessarily indirect. When Bloom wonders about the texture of his own body and the color of his own flesh (U 182, 375), he is engaged in a voyage of discovery, the discovery of the last novelty of all. Fear of bodily death, the great unfair surprise, produces literature, in Ulysses. The discovery of the body by the soul produces the material for literature, in the Wake.

In the Wake the maker constantly mates with the made, to produce the universe. There are only two characters in the Wake, Man and Woman, and even they are representations of the ultimate realities of Form and Matter. In Stephen Hero the young Joyce plays with 'a theory of dualism which would symbolize the twin eternities of spirit and nature in the twin eternities of male and female'.[12] Therefore, all the men in the book are Man, as all the women in the book are Woman. 'Shem and Shaun and the shame that sunders em' (FW 526), Tristan, the Norwegian Captain, HCE, the Twelve, the Four – these are all hypostatized stages of the life of Man. The stages, from Tristan onward, are easy to identify: Tristan the lover; the Norwegian Captain the swain, bridegroom and husband; HCE the father; the Twelve the man as citizen; the Four the man as senile, as thanatic grandfathers as systems of dusty experience. The first stage – 'Shem and Shaun and the shame that sunders em' – is mysterious. Certainly they represent the man as child and young man, but why are there two or three of them, and why are they so different?

> —Three in one, one and three.
> Shem and Shaun and the shame that sunders em.
> Wisdom's son, folly's brother.   (FW 526.13–15)

The relation of Shaun to Shem must be of importance in the *Wake* since most of Book III, half of the narrative portion of the text, is devoted to Shaun (if we assume that the 'narrative' occupies only Books II and III). Shaun seems to develop, change, mature and merge into HCE in the course of Book III. Book III contains the mysterious process of resurrection; HCE, whom we have seen destroyed in Book II, chapter 3, now stammers 'Here we are again' (*FW* 532.6–7). HCE is resurrected in Shaun by some method. Joyce, to show that he has not left Aquinas behind, insists upon a bodily resurrection as well as a spiritual; HCE's attempted sexual act in Book III, chapter 4, is followed by a description of the nuptial flight and, in Book IV, by a universal call to rise up. The growth of the body and the textures of the soul are intimately related, as we have seen in the description of Lipoti Virag. I contend that Books II, III and IV of the *Wake* contain a description of the physical integration of the parts of the immature male – the top half and the bottom half – to the point where he becomes mature. In other words, the *Wake* presents in fable form what *Portrait* and *Ulysses* present in naturalistic terms.

Shem and Shaun and the shame that sunders em

Book I of the *Wake*, which Joyce once described as an 'immense shadow',[13] gives us clues about Shem and Shaun that enable us to follow the development of their relationship in the narrative books, II and III. In the following analysis, I shall gather clues from Book I, and then trace the tale of the reconciliation of Shem and Shaun in Books II and III.

That Shem and Shaun represent male polar opposites has been obvious for a long time. However, Joyce distinguishes them clearly from each other by more than their opposition. Shem and Shaun represent at least one opposition of great importance to the theory of the male soul in Joyce: Shaun is the top half of the male body, and Shem is the bottom half. Shaun's embarrassment is the embarrassment of any decent top half when confronted by the unbridled and indecent behavior of his bottom half. Poor young Stephen Dedalus is terrified by the self-will and immorality of his own penis, in *Portrait*: 'The eyes see the thing, without having wished to see. Then in an instant it happens. But does that part of the body understand or what?' (*P* 139). The eyes, in the top half of the body, see; and the penis erects itself – how dreadful, thinks the frightened adolescent. Shaun is this frightened adolescent for most of Book II but gradually begins to come to terms with Shem in Book III, until the old Adam rises up in III. iii and ratifies the beginning of Shaun's manhood.

As we have seen, in the analysis of *Ulysses*, Joyce takes the claims of the body with complete seriousness. His rejection of Dublin Platonists was complete and final. Fear of the death of the body is the impetus behind creation. Indeed, Joyce takes the claims of the body so seriously that a reader may be embarrassed to follow him. An attitude of respect for *all* of the human physical envelope is easier to fake than to feel with sincerity. Even many emancipated readers feel a puritanical horror of the body; it is Shaun's horror of Shem they are feeling. Even Ezra Pound, the explosive artistic revolutionary, nervously counsels Joyce to tone down the scene of Bloom at stool.[14] The long-suppressed letters of Joyce to Nora are shocking in their insistence on the physical facts of the body. (They are more shocking, incidentally, than any of Joyce's works, because in these letters he was attempting a truly kinetic art.) Even I can only extend a critic's courtesy to Joyce on this matter – there is much of Shaun in me also.

The *Wake* consists of two parts – Book I, a 'great shadow', and Books II, III and IV, which present a temporal sequence from dusk to dawn. In Book I, fragments of the mature man are interspersed with fragments of the immature man, both disguised as characters in the dream. I shall gather the clues which are scattered widely through the first book and attempt to show how the nature of the developing male body is suggested in the text. Then with the beginning of the temporal sequence of the *Wake* I shall follow the integration of the male body as it occurs. We must not be surprised that Joyce disguises the top half and the bottom half as two complete people. We can find features of both halves in both Shem and Shaun, but even here there are strong indications that the two sons are really one man.

On the first page (*FW* 3.7) the hero is identified as 'topsawyer's rocks', a combination of topsawyer and rocks – top half and testicles. (The bottom-sawyer turns up at *FW* 173.28–9.) In *FW* 7.10–11, 29–30, the hero is described twice as a head-and-tail creature, a top and a bottom. In the Willingdone Museyroom episode, the light-and-dark motif joins the top-and-bottom one: Hinnessy the bright one is the top half; most male bottom halves are dark because they are concealed in trousers, so Dooley the dark one is Hinnessy's mate. It is at this point that the eventual method of cooperation of top and bottom is clearly foreshadowed; the two become three in one. Together, the two halves are the two testicles, with the Davy, later called 'the shame that sunders em', at first below them, then (incited by them, as the dormouse is incited by the March Hare and the Mad Hatter) rising above them to destroy the Willingdone. Sexual maturity of sons is feared by the father; it is the sign of his coming overthrow, his relegation to the role of *grand-père*, or Old King Mark. The three soldiers are the tripartite male sexual apparatus, as the two girls are the bi-symmetrical female genitals. Once the top half and the bottom half stop their feud (the 'bog lipoleum mordering the lipoleum beg', *FW* 8.24), they are capable of a mature erection of their 'shame that sunders em', and the overthrow of the old father. This is the great male battle, the father striving to keep his sons immature, the sons growing to become fathers. This is why HCE fears the liers-in-wait; time is on their side. The sexual sniper Buckley is going to shoot through the old Russian general sooner or later.

There are further scattered clues in I. i. Mutt and Jute add further details. Jute is quite articulate – after all, the top half has the mouth and the lungs. Mutt, however, is somewhat deaf ('deaf as your arse', an Irish expression: see *FW* 268.L4), and the bottom half can give utterance only in the bottom half's unfortunate broken-winded stuttering manner. In the Prankquean fable the hero pulls himself together, both burnt head and bruised heels, and establishes the family on an organized basis. The Prankquean assists him by introducing his halves to each other and forcing them to share each other's characteristics. At the end of I. i, on *FW* 27, Kevin's cherubic cheek is contrasted to nasty Jerry's playing with his leavings.

There is little on this matter in I. ii and I. iii. In these chapters Shem is described as a traveller from down under, Van Diemen's Land, at *FW* 56.20–1, thereby introducing the geographical motif. The lower half *is* 'down under', so Shem as Australian or Tasmanian or New Zealander/Maori is always threatening to rise up and return from exile. Indeed, as the Devil, he is as far down as anyone can get. The statement that 'there is not very much windy

Nous blowing at any given moment through the hat' of Shem is reasonable; Shem's wind does not blow through his hat, and it does not blow from the Nous but rather from Poldy's wind-instrument.

Aspects of the obscure Festy King trial scene in I. iv have considerable relevance to the top–bottom motif. The testimony of Festy, who is charged with 'making fesses' (FW 85.30), is interrupted by one of the thunder-words filled with references to sexual activity (FW 90.31–3), and again by an enormous breaking of wind (FW 92.8), after which Festy is immediately identified as Shem by the little girls. (However, there is some doubt about who is who in the trial. Surely the Wet Pinter is Shem in his urinating mode (FW 92.7).)

The Mamafesta chapter (I. v) has no prominent contributions to the motif until the very end – the question in Russian, 'How are you today, my dark sir?', with its answer, 'Shem the Penman' (FW 125.22–3). All of the greetings in this form in the Wake are probably mutual greetings of the top half greeting the bottom half – 'How are you today, my dark sir?' – and the bottom half greeting the top half – 'How are you today, my blond sir?' Man is trying to see if he is still all there after a night of intense and constant testing, disintegration and reintegration.

This question introduces a set of references to the motif. I. vi consists of questions addressed by Shem to Shaun. This is appropriate, since the top half has the vocal apparatus to answer the constantly embarrassing questions posed by the bottom half. The bottom half has a 'voice' of sorts, but most of its 'utterances' are songs without words.

Three questions contribute clues. The answer to Question 2 contains a reference to 'hot Hammurabi or cowld Clesiastes' as the two banks of Anna Livia, and as her fervent admirers (FW 139.25–6). They also represent state and church, of course, but the hot hams of Hammurabi and the cold cowl of the preacher conceal the bottom half of Shem and the top half of Shaun. Hammurabi and Clesiastes make up two-thirds of HCE, her husband. More than just the top half and bottom half of a male body make up a husband; the 'shame that sunders em' plays a vital part.

The answer to Question 10 shows Issy at her mock-innocent pursuit of inciting her twin brothers. However, the physical references are mixed, and detailed comment on her two-pronged attack will be found below.

The answer to Question 11 and the subsequent Shem chapter (I. vii) provide many amplifications and clarifications of the top–bottom motif. Question 11 itself provides some clues. Shem is an 'acheseyeld', with no teeth (he lisps) and a habit of breaking wind. As we will see, Shem has only one eye, and in this he represents the monocular penis (Eliot refers to this unsavory folk-tradition of 'old one-eye' in his use of the traditional ribald ballad of 'One-Eyed Riley', in *The Cocktail Party*). The habit of breaking wind and the toothless mouth signify the anus. Shaun's answer, therefore, is partly the horrified comments of the brain on the indignities of the genito-excretory system.

Shaun	Shem
Top half	*Bottom half*
voice – tenor, clear, unhesitating	'voice' – bass, stuttering
belches	farts
arms and hands	legs
static	kinetic
brain – analysis	genitals – synthesis
thinks and answers	reacts and questions
sadism	masochism
prefers fresh food	prefers 'processed' food
greedy and avaricious	generous
absorbs flow	gives out flow
violent	cowardly
clean and sweet-smelling	dirty and stinking
clear-sighted	one-eyed

Shaun's attack on time also here and throughout the *Wake* reflects his horror at his own bottom half. The time-space distinction is related in the *Wake* to the bottom-top distinction, but the roots of the distinction are to be found in *Ulysses*; the legs mark off time *nacheinander* in the 'Proteus' chapter, while the eyes, seated in the head, define space *nebeneinander*.

You are walking through it howsomever. I am, a stride at a time. A very short space of time through very short times of

space. Five, six: the *nacheinander*. . . . My two feet in his boots
are at the end of my legs *nebeneinander*.   (*U* 37)

The bottom half moves a great deal: the legs move, the penis
(uncannily) moves, the fluids and wastes emerge from the bottom
half. Motion is not the main occupation of the top half; in the top
half, only the arms and the features of the face move, and they
need not move at all, for much human activity, while the bottom
half moves constantly. Indeed, this foreshadows a further
development of the top-bottom motif: the top half greedily takes
in through the eyes, the ears, the nose and the mouth, and stores
what is has absorbed in the mind and in the stomach, while the
bottom half generously gives out material and fluid through the
action of the genito-excretory system and, by the actions of the
legs, moves kinetically to effect what the brain has desired.

The Fable of the Mookse and the Gripes acquires an extra
dimension when interpreted from the angle of the top–bottom
motif. The Mookse, proud but unstable (it walks with a stick),
confronts its genitals, the Gripes, hanging downward from a limb.
The Mookse lacks definitive male sexuality, as the 'moo-cow'
element of his appellation suggests. The Gripes's reference to him
as 'loudy bullocker' (*FW* 154.33–4) reinforces the notion of the
Mookse as lacking genitals, and the Mookse's sword is a shattered
lance (*lanzia spezzata*). Indeed, the name of Breakspear borne by
the papal version of the Mookse suggests sexual incapacity. The
Gripes is the Mookse's sexual capacity, even in physical appearance. Joyce may also be suggesting in this symbolic dichotomy
the inability of the church to function without the aid of the Irish
clergy:

> 'Tis Irish brains that save from doom
> The leaky barge of the Bishop of Rome
> For everyone knows the Pope can't belch
> Without the consent of Billy Walsh.
> ('Gas from a Burner', ll. 21–4)[15]

There is a good deal of further evidence in the text that one of
the important themes of the fable is the top-bottom motif. The
Mookse cares for and dresses the upper portion of his body – eyes,
nostrils, ears and throat (*FW* 152.23–4). Although he can walk,
his gait is probably impeded by his father's broken lance between

his legs (*FW* 156.31–2). The Gripes is 'bolt downright', and is called a 'brooder-on-low'; from the point of view of the apprehensive top half, the bottom half, especially the genitals, must seem to be brooding in the dark, hatching out evil plans (*FW* 153.10–11, 18–19).

The Gripes wishes the Mookse 'good appetite', appropriate words when addressed to the half that contains the mouth (*FW* 153.35). The Mookse blasts the Gripes for his 'anathomy in-fairioriboos', the lower anatomy (*FW* 154.11). The bellowing voice of the Mookse comes from the mouth, while the cheeping, whining tones of the Gripes derives from other orifices. '*Culla vosellina*' may mean 'in a little voice' in Italian dialect, but it suggests other, more basic meanings.[16]

The Mookse loftily declares that 'I can seen from my holeydome what it is to be wholly sane' (*FW* 155.15–16). This statement should be recalled when reading Shaun's contention that Shem is mad (*FW* 193.28); the brain believes that any organ outside itself is not sane, certainly not the irresponsible genitals.

The Mookse reads a great deal, as one might expect from the half that contains the eyes (*FW* 155.32–6; 156.1–7). (Curiously, Shem the Penman *writes* a great deal, but does he ever *read* anything? His 'pen' is surely the penis, but Shaun has the hands to hold the pen.)

The Mookse is beautifully groomed, perfumed with Yardley's cologne, and bears a military haircut, but his feet hurt (as Shaun's will hurt) (*FW* 156.28–30). Shaun's sadism, the sexual preference of the top half, is suggested by 'as british as bondstrict'; in Book III we see Shaun constantly threatening sadistic violence to Issy. Sadism is the only form of sexual outlet for the top half, the half with the arms.

The Gripes is suffering from halitosis or worse, as we might expect (*FW* 156.35–6). The odors associated with the bottom half disgust and frighten the top half. Nuvoletta cannot reconcile the halves; they can only come together with maturity. 'Let you be Beeton. And let me be Los Angeles,' declares the sadistic, intolerant Mookse (*FW* 154.23–4). Human beings cannot be entirely angels (the church defines a class of heresies as Angelism); they have bottoms also, but it is not the Gripes's bottom that will be 'Beeton' but Everyman's (see *FW* 564.23–5).

Even the final disposal of the Mookse and the Gripes follows the top–bottom pattern. *Aquila Rapax* is the name of the Mookse's final destination; the eagle carries him high. *De Rore Coeli* is where the Gripes ends up; he descends like the dew from heaven.[17]

The medieval form of debate between the body and the soul is transformed by Joyce into a comic dialogue of the top half of the body with the bottom half. Joyce seems to feel that the bottom half has not received its fair share of attention. However, the growth of the soul depends crucially upon a coming to terms between the two halves of the body. In the Fable of the Mookse and the Gripes, neither quarreller is mature; they are both Time's sons. At the end of the chapter, Time, in the words of the hymn, 'like an ever-flowing stream / Bears all its sons away' (*FW* 158.25–36; 159.1–5). However, at the end of the *Wake* the river of Time sees her husband looming up like the sun over Ben Howth and bearing down on her – she will not carry the mature man away.

The Fable of Burrus and Caseous adds little to what we have already found. The stinking cheese is viewed with disgust by the sweet butter, but, unfortunately for the forces of decency, the lovely Margareena is fond of both. Women have a disconcerting way of preferring complete men as their consorts, so Margareena chooses Antonius, who bears the characteristics of both Burrus and Caseous (*FW* 167.1–3).

The Shaun answer ends with the mouth praising its own breath and its own words:

> My unchanging Word is sacred. The word is my Wife, to expense and expound, to vend and to velnerate, and may the curlews crown our nuptias. Till Breath us depart. Wamen.
>
> (*FW* 167.28–31)

However, the Breath has only paused to take breath, before launching into a violent attack on the Tail.

The sustained invective of the Shem chapter sets Time flowing in the *Wake*. What looks first like a mere extension of the last two questions in I. vi turns into the transition to the Anna Livia chapter (I. viii), which itself begins the flow of narrative time, moving from dusk to dawn in Books II and III. The Shem chapter is therefore the point in the *Wake* in which paradigma becomes syntagma, where structure becomes system. If Shaun and Shem do indeed represent the top and bottom halves of the body, the narrative text of the *Wake* begins to flow when the body of man is united as Justius and Mercius. Maturity is the precondition for male creativity, and the acceptance of the organs of outflow by the greedy avaricious brain is the precondition for maturity. It is perhaps too much to say that Shaun enthusiastically accepts Shem, but his flailing, all-out assault upon his brother causes Mercius to begin to flow. Shaun's vigorous oral outflow is aided by Shem – how could it be otherwise? The mouth is Shaun's; the flow is Shem's. Shaun asks openly for assistance at one point (*FW* 191.1–2), but it is a fair guess that Shem is helping him all the time in I. vii as a result of the union effected by the twelfth question in I. vi:

> 12. *Sacer esto?*
> Answer: *Semus sumus!*   (*FW* 168.13–14)

'We are Shem' marks the union of the halves; the Shem chapter displays the mouth flowing with language contributed by the lower centres (by Lipoti Virag) on the subject of the embarrassing nature of the male body and, ultimately, on the nature of time and language. When Mercius finally reinforces Justius he produces three phrases, of which the third is an enormously long ejaculation, a single sentence forty-five lines long. In this sentence, a triumph of cantilevered syntax, Mercius declares that 'it is to you, . . . to me, . . . you alone, . . . to me . . . that our turf brown mummy is acoming, . . . giddygaddy, grannyma, gossipaceous Anna Livia' (*FW* 194.12–13, 14, 16, 22; 195.3–4). The unified body produces language as a revivifying seminal fluid – what the maker has made – producing orgasm in the body of Time, and constantly fertilizing what else the maker has made, the matter of the world, Anna Livia, and producing the world developing in Time. An act of superfetation, Eliot and the mystic theologians would call it. When the body becomes unified, in Book IV, the act of fertilization is completed.

The configurations of Shem in I. vii reveal very little that is new: Shem is the lower, dark half viewed with alarm by the top sunny half. There is some attempt to make Shem a complete human being, with many bottom-half and some top-half features: he is credited with a skull, shoulders, ears and thumbs, among other details (*FW* 169.11, 15, 16–17), but many of the top-half details could be interpreted as bottom-half features: his 'larkseye' could be the monocular penis (*FW* 169.12; see also *FW* 174.19,

182.6, 33–4); indeed, the text says explicitly 'the simian has no sentiment secretion' (*FW* 192.22–3). 'The whoel of a nose' could be the nether 'whoel' (*FW* 169.12); 'one numb arm up a sleeve' could be the penis itself (*FW* 169.12–13); and his hair and beard could be equally superior and inferior areas.

The 'lowness' of Shem, repeated in various forms twenty-one times in twenty-two pages,[18] provides the most explicit description of Shem as bottom half. Moral lowness is conflated with his general symbolic lowness. The bottom-half status of Shem also explains his taste in food. He enjoys food that has been preserved in tins rather than the fresh equivalent because, by the time food reaches the lower half of the body, a great deal of alteration has taken place. Shaun, the mouth, prefers fresh, or freshly killed, meat or fish. Shem's drinking habits are also conditioned by lowness – he drinks wine, perhaps because grapes hang down (like the Gripes); Shaun's drinks are made from grain – 'firewater', 'firstshot', 'gin' or 'beer' (*FW* 171.13–14) – made from plants that grow up from the ground.[19] Shem's favorite drink resembles urine, the urine of an archduchess (*FW* 171.23–8).[20] Shaun suggests that heavenly love, Venus Urania, has been transformed by the low Shem into 'Fanny Urinia' (*FW* 171.28).

Of course, it is obvious to 'the Tulloch-Turnbull girl' that Shem is 'a bad fast man' by his 'walk', and the gypsy words he greets her with reinforce his image as a roamer. Equally, Shem cannot kill himself because most means of suicide involve the upper half; the four means suggested by Shaun all involve 'the cerebrum', or the lungs (drowning in Liffey, or 'pneumantics'), or suffocation by other means ('saffrocake') (*FW* 172.18–20). In addition, Shem is cowardly in other ways, because the legs are pre-eminently the organs of flight. While the eyes (of Shaun) are glaring aggressively at his adversaries during the First World War, the legs (of Shem) carry him to his Inkbottle House, where he lies in bed while his nether 'cheeks and his trousers change color for fear' (*FW* 177.6–7).

The odoriferous and excretory aspects of Shem are referred to several times. Shem will not be able to play 'non-excretory' games (*FW* 175.31); he is called a 'shit', and his 'Cloaxity' is one of the items for which Shaun (who has the nose) reproaches him (*FW* 179.6, 14). Shem's abominable smell disgusts all cookmaids; his 'stinksome inkenstink' is personal to the writer (*FW* 181.10–12;

183.6–7). His construction of ink from his own wastes (*FW* 185.6–33) is only appropriate; the 'squidself' that he creates is made of ink – squid's ink is ejected from an orifice near its anus (*FW* 186.6–7).

Shem's darkness is referred to, mainly by making him black (*FW* 175.30; 177.4), while Shaun's sunny blondness is brought up, perhaps to contrast (*FW* 186.17–18; 187.2). Another contrast: Shaun burps and hiccups (*FW* 177.31, 32, 33) as opposed to Shem's wind-breaking.

The Justius tirade is the first time that Shaun's direct view of his own bottom half produces a seminal flow (the definitive time is of course in III. ii, when Shaun produces the rise of Dave the Dancekerl). In the Justius section, the main characteristics of Shem are recapitulated: his darkness (blackness), his doubtful cleanliness (esp. *FW* 188.4–6, 12), his constant motions, his lowness, his madness. Shaun's own characteristics emerge clearly from the tirade – the brawn of his arms and the broadness of his brow, and violence associated with the arms (*FW* 187.24–7), his whiteness and purity (*FW* 188.12; 191.13–28). Shaun's violence acquires a larger dimension with *FW* 190.1–9:

> it never stphruck your mudhead's obtundity . . . that the more carrots you chop, the more turnips you slit, the more murphies you peel, the more onions you cry over, the more bullbeef you butch, the more mutton you crackerhack, the more potherbs you pound, the fiercer the fire and the longer your spoon and the harder you gruel with more grease to your elbow the merrier fumes your new Irish stew.

This passage expresses more than the gluttony of the mouth; it is a defence of political violence. 'Turnips' are not usually 'slit' for Irish stew, but 'turnups' (trouser cuffs) are slit as part of the ritual for execution in the electric chair. Potatoes are peeled for stew, but here the reference is also to Irishmen attacked by 'peelers', policemen. The 'bullbeef' that is butchered can be British soldiers killed by Irish rebels. Shaun seems to realize that his new Irish stew, the revolution beginning with Easter Week, is a supping with the Devil (traditionally, one uses 'a long spoon' to sup with the Devil), but he defends the use of violence in political matters, knowing that the cowardly bottom half would not approve (see also *FW* 411.24–5 for Shaun as a practitioner of political violence).

Shem's personality acquires some new aspects in the Justius section. Shem's religious doubts are expressed, significantly as 'you have become of twosome twiminds forenenst gods, . . . nay, . . . you have reared your disunited kingdom on the vacuum of your own most intensely doubtful soul' (*FW* 188. 14–17). The double nature of the bottom half – man as a poor forked creature – communicates itself to the mind, which also becomes double and mobile. (Previously, Shem had prayed to 'the cloud Incertitude' (*FW* 178.31–2); subsequently, Mercius thanks 'Movies' (*FW* 194.2) from the depths of his heart.)

Finally, Shaun pokes openly at Shem's (his own) genitals, after apologizing to all, and reproaches Shem, who avoids his duty to be fruitful and multiply, and instead pours out words on paper (*FW* 188.20–36; 189.1–10). Oddly enough, the literal genitals conceal a symbolic meaning here; previously, the genitals had been presented symbolically. Shaun's gross description of the 'selfraising syringe and twin feeders' describes the mental organization of a writer. The description harks back to some of Joyce's earliest writing:

> The artist, he [Stephen] imagined, standing in the position of mediator between the world of his experience and the world of his dreams – «a mediator, consequently, gifted with twin faculties, a selective faculty and a reproductive faculty.» To equate these faculties was the secret of artistic success: the artist who could disentangle the subtle soul of the image from its mesh of defining circumstances most exactly and «re-rembody» it in artistic circumstances chosen as the most exact for it in its new office, he was the supreme artist.
>
> (*Stephen Hero* 77–8)

The 'twin faculties' of *Stephen Hero* become the 'twin feeders' of Justius, and the 'artist-mediator' of *Stephen Hero* is the 'selfraising syringe' of the crass Shaun. In both texts the artistic creation is metaphorically conveyed as a material creation, a 're-embodying' of the world in another form. No wonder Shaun accuses Shem of scribbling with the penis instead of populating the world with it! It is completely Joycean to provide a delicate psychological interpretation for a gross physical fact; so often, he provides just the opposite.

Shem, it appears, has incited pure Shaun to masturbation, an art which elucidates II. ii and III. ii: 'him [Shaun] you laid low with one hand one find May morning . . . (not one did you slay, no, but a continent!)' (FW 191.28–9, 31). Shaun's hand was taken over by the spirit of Shem, who then 'impossibilises' (U 389) many thousands of life-possibilities by self-abuse (FW 183.3) and turns a 'continent' being into an incontinent one.

Mercius, who begins the flowing of Time and Anna Livia, bears some of the characteristics of Shem: the blackness (FW 193.34 – combined with evil – the 'black mass'), and the secrecy, the natural concealing of the genitals by the sense of decency ('unseen blusher in an obscene coalhole, the cubilibum of your secret sigh' (FW 194.18–19), and the uncertainty of the mobile and divided principle (FW 193.35–6). Mainly, Mercius is the entire male body sexually aroused, because the pronouns in the Mercius passage alternate between 'I' and 'you', It is the male body and soul prepared for creation, and causing the creation of narrative: 'He lifts the lifewand and the dumb speak' (FW 195.5). 'Movies' are beginning at this point. Justius has previously created a series of still pictures from ever-flowing reality (FW 193.29 – 'the quick are still'); Mercius gives continuous sound to the series of stills and begins the projector. At first the sound-projector moves slowly, and the first sound, 'O' in I. viii, comes out as 'Quoiquoiquoiquoiquoiquoiquoiquoiq!' However, the projector soon speeds up sufficiently to produce 'O' and the rest of the Anna Livia chapter. The speed of the projection increases gradually throughout I. viii, but the flickering image never gets swift enough in the chapter to produce more than a twilight; the illusion of reality begins with 'The Mime of Mick, Nick and the Maggies'. However, it is because of Mercius, the excited male body, that 'our mummy is coming', in the form of an orgasmic flow of narrative and life.

* * *

At the end of Book I, Justius and Mercius begin pouring out Anna Livia, and the narrative is about to begin. It may seem odd that sons give birth to their mother, and yet this is orthodox: Dante testifies to this in *figlia del tuo figlio*. Justice and Mercy are the attributes of the creative lord of all, and Time flows from his plenitude. ('From forth of his pierced part comes the woman of his dreams', FW 78.32.) It is also the turn of the tide – the Liffey is an estuary in Dublin, and the waters here begin their flow to the sea, which will end in Book IV. On the maternal-paternal tide of time floats the family, downstream to its consummation.

Books II, III and IV, the temporal books, represent, among many other themes, the growth to sexual maturity of the young men and women and the overthrow of the old. From dusk Angelus through midnight 'Angelus' till dawn Angelus the young man discovers himself, the young woman discovers the young man (top half and bottom half), and the transfer of potency is made from the old to the young. After some sexual failures, there is a spectacular sexual success which ends the *Wake* and begins it.

Book II presents the development of the children to sexual maturity; Book III presents the growth of the young man to the threshold of the husband's estate, and the passing from that estate of the old man. Book IV presents the arrival of the new mature man and his new mature wife.

Book II, chapter 1, presents the very young children beginning to discover themselves. Shaun is the pure innocent we have met, the sweet aspects of the body beloved by his young female playfellows. The worship of the solar Shaun (*FW* 234.6–239.29) involves his cleanliness, his smile, his loose curls, his tender eye-glances, his glory, his sweetness and his purity. Unlike lower-half Shem, he has not 'brought stinking members' into the house of love (*FW* 237.26). His intercourse with the little flowers opening up to him 'does not defile' (*FW* 237.23–4). His head and face are touched by the cosmetic goddesses. He is, in other words, a pure top half of a male body. He is the spirit of gaiety, singing gay songs of a French cast in a high tenor voice (*FW* 222.7–9). However, there are hints that his sexual activity is based on sadism, a hint which will be developed further in III. ii: at *FW* 232.19, Issy complains (to Shem) that she has 'soreunder' from Shaun. The top half is the half of sadism; the bottom half (as Bloom could testify) is the realm of masochism.

Shem, as usual, is 'foulend up' (*FW* 239.35), and involved in the underworld. Shem here is discovering the magic power of physical love, and in the course of his game he infects Issy with his black sorcery (*FW* 250.23–7). The answer to the third question, which the text suggests he has failed to answer (*FW* 253.19), is followed by Issy's rebellion, and her suggestive songs about her father, for which she is spanked and pulled indoors. However, it is too late to reverse Shem's black magic – 'a burning would has come to dance inane' (*FW* 250.16) – a 'would' is a tentative 'will', and a 'will' is a sexual drive or sexual organ, to the Elizabethans. This burning 'would' dances in Issy's 'inane' and excites her violently. Her father reacts powerfully in fear and rage, but it is too late; the process which will lead to his overthrow in II. iii is under way.

Book II, chapter 2, involves Shaun in the dangerous sexual game. Shem tricks his pure top half into knowledge of physical sexual fact. At *FW* 287.18 the text-river broadens out to the margins and baptizes her son; when the river returns to its banks the sexual diagram is revealed and the sons have crossed sides, sharing each other's knowledge, as in the Prankquean fable; the mother has constructed the complete body of man, as Isis assembled the lost limbs of Osiris, so that he may rise in the morning as Horus. Shaun is furious at the unwanted knowledge of himself forced on him by his mad, too knowledgeable bottom half, but finally accepts it, and both the high-up and low-down (*FW* 296.13–19), with their eyes open (*FW* 302.11–303.14), join with their sister in an ominous night-letter to their parents, containing threats which will be fulfilled in III. iii.

In III. iii Shem rises up from down under (warlike New Zealand warcries, *FW* 335.4–23) after the gentle Norwegian Captain has married the tailor's daughter. The risen phallus is a destructive weapon in the Buckley story, and in the Nightingale's song the castration of the father is referred to openly. The old order pulls itself together for a show of force, but it is too late. The mob of matured children rush up the straining stairs and crucify the old father (*FW* 371.2–380.5). Only the old feeble Roderick O'Connor is left. In the next chapter, II. iv, Tristan and Isolde copulate happily, while old age lies in the hold of their marriage bark.

Therefore, Book II presents the rise of the new order and death of the old. The midnight Angelus (*FW* 379.27–30) marks the shift of power in the family. As is usual with Joyce, one's rise is another's fall.

Now in Book III one's fall is another's rise. Book III is a great enigma. In one respect a clear series of chapters, in another it is puzzling – what happens to Shaun in it? Some close analysis will show that Book III contains a mystery greater than death – resurrection.

Physical maturity is reached at the end of Book II by both boy and girl – Tristan and Isolde have no difficulty in consummating a physical union with all the crass verve of a football game. But no reader of Joyce needs to be told that physical maturity is only the prelude to a full maturity, which it sometimes fails to attain – consider Little Chandler, Maria, Farrington, Eveline, James Duffy, Gabriel Conroy, young Stephen Dedalus. There is a mysterious further step to take before the light dawns, or is forcibly released by an ashplant-sword.

III. i and III. iv are framed by the bedroom of the aging couple. At the beginning of III. i the battered HCE in bed with ALP is having a nightmare. Reacting to his overthrow in Book II, he seems to be dreaming that a demon is about to take away his 'Anastashie', his resurrection as well as his wife. He dreams that the beaked, staring, bluetoothed, hornyhided black demon is gazing hungrily and coveting ALP. The demon is a dangerous African warrior (Jugurtha), hence probably (in Joycean symbolism) black; however, he is also Gogarty (('Gugurtha! Gugurtha!'), who perhaps may have had designs on Nora (*FW* 403.6–17)). The demon's thoughts ('Pensée!') are that ALP is the most beautiful woman in the world and would make a dainty morsel: 'She would stick to the vault of my palate,' hungrily thinks the demon, in HCE's uneasy nightmare. 'Avaunt,' thinks HCE, partly rousing himself from sleep, but the demon will not go away. The demon is the rising son, who will supersede HCE and become the new HCE in the course of Books III and IV.

HCE returns to his uneasy slumbers. (It is clear to me that it is the aging HCE because of his quotation of 'When you and I were young, Maggie' (*FW* 403.19).) His dreams occupy the rest of III. i, and also III. ii, III. iii and much of III. iv.

The interview of the ass with Shaun occupies the rest of III. i. In III. i, Shaun has not yet accepted the Shem half of himself, despite the callow copulation with Isolde in II. iv. He is described in great detail – but only down to the waist (*FW* 404.15–33). The only articles of clothing that apparel the dangerous areas are his shoes and his trouser-cuffs (but not the trousers themselves). He has barely accepted the fact that his feet are part of himself – he is always complaining of them and falling off them. He does not acknowledge his bottom or genitals at all in III. i. Perhaps his bottom and genitals are addressing him in the form of the sly cunning ass that questions him. If so, the situation in III. i is just that of the Mookse and the Gripes, with the hugely developed and pompous top half unsteadily balancing itself on its unacknowledged bottom half (in III. ii and III. iii Shaun, like the Mookse, requires a cane to walk upright (*FW* 445.14; 474.3–4)), and trying to ignore the excitations and embarrassing questions raised by his dangerous areas.

The Shaun we have become acquainted with is before us in detail in III. i. His eating is enormous, but his hunger is even greater (*FW* 405.17–407.9, 422.24–6), and his voice is lovely (*FW* 407.13–28, 412.7–9), although occasionally he hiccups (*FW* 423.10–14). In addition to such top-half features as mouth, stomach and vocal apparatus, he is also proud of his brain (as are the Mookse and Professor Jones) – he is quite confident he can read Greek and many other languages (*FW* 419.20–7). His sadism (*FW* 421.30–1) and violence are also present – there is a hint that he was responsible for Easter Week and the subsequent violence (*FW* 411.22–3). He is also bigoted – he would burn all pornographers (*FW* 426.1–4) in the name of defending his mother.

Although in III. ii and III. iii his mood will soften as he begins to accept all aspects of himself, in III. i he is still furious with Shem. Therefore, he accepts with alacrity the ass's ironic suggestions that the body of Shaun is made of a tinted cloud, a notion derived from the heretical Valentinian (d.c. 160), who in *Ulysses* is described as having 'spurned Christ's terrene body' (*U* 21). Shaun is obviously pleased with the notion that he has a 'softbodied fumiform' (*FW* 413.31). He also embraces the notion of significant form, a form without content, which is a notion associated with Roger Fry (see *FW* 413.24, 35). Shaun is only at the first stage of mature acceptance of himself.

Shem is not much in evidence. In Book III he is hidden away inside trousers and nightgowns until various crucial moments. In III. i he possesses the bottom half's characteristic imprudent attitudes and its skill in dancing (*FW* 414.22–415.15). (The Ondt is more static, usually contenting himself with making faces at himself.) Shem's turn is coming, however.

In III. ii Shaun comes closer to accepting Shem. In fact, all of III. ii can be seen as an attempt by Shaun to excite himself into an erection, which he finally succeeds in doing. However, neither the erection in III. ii nor the ones in III. iii and III. iv produce definitive results; that is reserved for Book IV.

In III. i Shaun denies the presence of his genitals. In III. ii they are in their appropriate place; the little girls in the nightschool rush at him and are 'jingaling his jellybags for, though he looked a young chapplie of sixtine, they could frole by his manhood that he was just the killingest ladykiller all by kindness' (*FW* 430.30–3). This is certainly an advance upon the young Shaun, who struck his brother for introducing him to the physical facts of life, or upon the Shaun who preferred to be a 'softbodied fumiform'; here at least is the equipment.

Characteristically, however, Shaun attempts to excite himself into ejaculation by sadistic fantasies and furious prurient rhetoric. This is 'sex in the head', indeed (to quote a writer that Joyce regarded with suspicion). Sadism runs through the entire sermon to the young girls (*FW* 432.31; 436.33–437.1; 439.3–4; 444.17–24; 445.1–25). In the course of his inflammatory sermon Shaun attempts to achieve 'sadisfaction', but it is only when Issy joins in and assists him (*FW* 457.25–461.32) that erection is achieved. With a cry of 'MEN!' Shaun achieves his erection; Dave the Dancekerl rises up from down under, with his odor, convict's shaven crown, 'testymonicals', single eye (*FW* 464.12), 'penals' (*FW* 465.5), low voice (*FW* 466.31–467.8), and all the other characteristics of the phallic Shem. However, the sadistically induced erection produces no useful ejaculation:

> do you twig the schamlooking leaf greeping ghastly down his
> blousyfrock? Our national umbloom! Areesh! He won't. He's
> shoy.   (*FW* 467.10–12)

Masturbation – whether mental or physical – is not an act of complete sexual maturity. Here Joyce also seems to be referring to a specifically Irish debility – the 'schamlooking' emblem of a paralyzed Ireland, an Ireland whose sexual drives were perhaps killed by the Famine; in *Ulysses*, Old Gummy Granny wears 'the deathflower of the potato blight on her breast' (*U* 595).

Shaun then departs after falling off his unsteady feet but there are definite intimations of coming sunrise, when the heavenly marriage will finally be consummated.

In III. iii the four old men dig through the layers of the comatose Shaun. After much evasion, HCE emerges, with a giant poem to his own creation, civilization in the form of cities. It is possible to see the resurrection of HCE as an erection, Nelson's Pillar in the center of Dublin. In 'Aeolus', the city traffic swirls around the Pillar (*U* 116), as it does at the end of 'Haveth Childers Everywhere' (*FW* 553.28–554.9). Nelson's Pillar is more likely to be the phallus of the sleeping giant who extends from Howth to Castleknock than is the Wellington obelisk. In addition, this notion elucidates Stephen's 'Pisgah Sight of Palestine'; two aged creatures produce a feeble flow of seeds from the top of a phallic monument to an adulterer. Surely it does not require a particularly devious mind to see in 'Aeolus' the male genital apparatus feebly at work. (And now the phallic pillar is gone – poor Dublin!) In III. iii the phallus is again erected, here as the creative sign of the city-creator. The city and the erected phallus are designed for the pleasure of ALP, and she is seen exulting in her joy at the close of the chapter.

However, this is only in a dream, and in III. iv the sexual attempt by the aging HCE, though overseen by church and state (canon law and civil law) (*FW* 572.19–576.9), is infertile. He wears a contraceptive, and never wets the tea. Like his son in III. ii, HCE fails to complete the heavenly act of love with the earth. This suggests that the nuptial flight of the queen-bee at the close of III. iv is an anticipation of the successful act of love in Book IV.

Book IV is pervaded with sunlight and happiness. The rising of the new sun is the advent of the complete man, finally, and is hailed by all the news-services, King Leary erupts from the viceking's mound, St Patrick defends the visible-audible-gnosible world, and the sun-worshippers praise the source of all outward reality. At the end of Book IV, and of the *Wake*, Anna Livia flows out to sea. The Liffey is an estuary in Dublin, and the sea current turns the tide periodically. First the Liffey flows out to sea; then the sea backs the Liffey up, periodically, in a sexual rhythm, for ever. At the end of the *Wake* the tide has not yet turned, and Anna Livia flows outward, dying, with the last of her orgasm, which was begun with Mercius. On the last page of the *Wake*, Anna Livia sees the sun over the bar in Dublin Bay (*FW* 607.30) since she flows directly eastward. She sees her husband rising over Howth, on widespread white solar wings, like an archangel. She feels the tide turning – 'I'm getting mixed' – 'Brightening up and tightening down' – the seawater is entering her and turning her tide. At 'Us, then!' the tide turns, she dies at the turn of the tide (she 'dies' in the Elizabethan sense at the

Mercius episode), and the last sentence begins the rhythm of the sexual penetration of the sea – 'A way a long a last a loved a long the' – she feels herself loved and she feels the entrance of her lover, 'Sir Tristram, violer d'amores', who has just 'rearrived' from the east 'to wielderfight his penisolate war'. Here at last is the successful act of love. When the reader returns to Book I the Liffey is flowing backwards – 'past Eve and Adam's', not 'Adam and Eve's' – and she continues to flow backwards all through Book I, until in I. vii Mercius declares that Anna Livia is 'coming', and her orgasm produces the whole narrative in Books II and III.

The rhythm of the *Wake* is sexual, therefore, and one of the basic stories of the *Wake* is the integration of the male body. The marriage of heaven and earth, of form and matter, is celebrated in the *Wake*, after a series of unsuccessful or immature attempts, and the production of the world from the integrated body of man is described.[21]

Joyce produces two explanations of creation, one in *Ulysses* and one in the *Wake*. In *Ulysses* the fundamental drives symbolized by Lipoti Virag are the sources of language. However, Lipoti is motivated by the fear of bodily death, and therefore creation is a reaction to the threat of extinction. In the *Wake*, on the other hand, creation – the mating of heaven and earth – is the result of bodily integration, the reconciliation of Shem and Shaun.

This is not a contradiction; Joyce has provided a combined answer to questions about the soul of man: in the works of Joyce, the world is constantly produced by death and resurrection of the body.

Notes

1 The whole 'Circe' chapter is laced with hallucination, magic and metaphor, but there are thirteen major hallucinatory metaphors interspersed with naturalistic dialogue in real time. These episodes actually interrupt the action and stop time until they are finished:

1 *U* 437–41 *Rudolph Bloom (father)*
2 *U* 442–9
3 *U* 453–74
4 *U* 478–99
5 *U* 505–10
6 *U* 511–23 *Lipoti Virag*
7 *U* 523–5
8 *U* 527–54

     9 *U* 563-9
    10 *U* 572-4
    11 *U* 579-83
    12 *U* 598-600
    13 *U* 609   *Rudolph Bloom (son)*

Nine of the episodes are centered on Bloom. Only four (7, 10, 11 and 12) are centered on Stephen; that is, of the 114 pages devoted to major hallucinations, only ten pages are centered on Stephen. However, the pattern of the hallucinations is Bloom to Stephen; Bloom solves most of his emotional problems before Stephen fails to solve his (in 10, 11 and 12). Another unexpected regularity is found by comparing 1 with 13: the first major hallucinatory figure is Rudolph Bloom, Bloom's father; the last hallucinatory figure is Rudolph Bloom, Bloom's son. Lipoti Virag, Bloom's grandfather-goblin in 6, occurs between these figures (*exactly* between, in terms of pages).

2   Sometimes, however, they are responses to material within hallucination.

3   Zoe, from Greek *zoion*, living being, animal, as opposed to Greek *bios*, life, mode of life. Both, however, derive from Indo-European **gwei*, by different routes (*American Heritage Dictionary*).

4   According to preliminary sketches for *Ulysses*, Lipoti Virag was originally not Bloom's grandfather at all but, as 'Litpold Virag', was a version of Henry Flower, then 'Bloom's double', and only then Bloom's grandfather. (See Phillip Herring (ed.), *Joyce's Notes and Early Drafts for Ulysses: Selection from the Buffalo Collection* (hereafter Herring, *Notes*) (Charlottesville, Virginia, University Press of Virginia, 1977), pp. 200, 225 (quoting *Ulysses*, Item V.A. 19, an early draft of 'Circe').) In other early drafts, he is called 'Leopold Peter', and his father is called 'Peter Rudolph'. (See Herring, *Notes*, p. 152; see also Phillip Herring (ed.), *Joyce's Ulysses Notesheets in the British Museum* (hereafter Herring, *Notesheets*) (Charlottesville, Virginia, University Press of Virginia, 1972), p. 100.)

5   See also *U* 606. Rudolph and Lipoti are referred to as being photographed by their '(respectively 1st and 2nd cousin, Stefan Virag' (*U* 723). This may be a mistake on Joyce's part; the family lines would have to be extremely complex for this to be accurate.

     Leopold Bloom is referred to as 'Lipoti Virag' on *U* 342, as part of his Hungarian farewell in the 'Cyclops' section. This reinforces the association of Bloom with Lipoti, but 'Lipoti Virag' just means 'Leopold Bloom (Flower)' in Hungarian.

6   For references to Sisyphus, see Herring, *Notesheets*, pp. 278, 284; Herring, *Notes*, p. 30; see also *U* 587, where Lynch is referred to as Sisyphus; Sisyphus was a notorious escaper, and Lynch is about to make his getaway. But Sisyphus as the son of the verbally creative Aeolus also receives mention: 'Poetic, neopoetic'.

7   The Homeric analogues for Lipoti Virag acquire an unexpected reinforcement from the genealogy of Bloom as Messiah, in *U* 495-6. The last three items of the heterogeneous list, corresponding in the real world to Lipoti, Rudolph and Leopold Bloom, are *Szombathely, Virag and Bloom*. Joyce seems

to have chosen Szombathely, an otherwise obscure town in western Hungary, as the dwelling-place of Bloom's ancestors, for the sound of its name; in Hungarian the name 'Szombathely' sounds almost exactly like the word 'somebody'. Lipoti Virag is, therefore, 'Mr Somebody', the grandfather of 'Mr Nobody', Ulysses himself.

8 Thoth is the Egyptian Hermes as Hermes Trismegistus, the scribe of the gods. He was a 'birdgod'; he bears the head of an ibis. The dog-headed baboon, sacred to Thoth, is mentioned in *U* 521.

9 Note that the dog does not belong to the Citizen; it is 'grandpapa Giltrap's lovely dog Garryowen' (*U* 352). So this is why the Citizen is roaming about with another man's dog – it is the dog of a 'grandpapa'!

10 Mark Shechner, in *Joyce in Nighttown: A Psychoanalytic Inquiry into Ulysses* (Berkeley, Cal., University of California Press, 1974), discusses Lipoti Virag briefly (pp. 110–11), but does not comment on his symbolic significance in either the Freudian schema of the personality or the Joycean.

11 For Freud, Eros represents the establishment and preservation of unities, and Thanatos (or the destructive instinct) represents the destruction of connections and the reduction of organic structures to inorganic states. The Joycean schema reverses this order – Eros embraces novelty, and Thanatos freezes novelty into pre-existing schemata. However, both Freud and Joyce postulate an intimate association between somatic structures and psychic processes. See S. Freud, *An Outline of Psychoanalysis*, trans. J. Strachey (New York, W. W. Norton, 1949), pp. 19–24, and *Beyond the Pleasure Principle*, in *The Standard Edition of the Complete Psychological Works of Sigmund Freud*, vol. XVIII (New York and London, Liveright Publishing Company and the Hogarth Press, 1955), pp. 36–42.

12 See E. L. Epstein, *The Ordeal of Stephen Dedalus* (Carbondale, Ill., Southern Illinois University Press, 1971), pp. 2–24, esp. pp. 22–3.

13 Breon Mitchell, 'Marginalia from Conversations with Joyce', *A Wake Digest*, ed. C. Hart and F. Senn (Sydney, Sydney University Press, 1968), p. 81.

14 *Pound/Joyce: The Letters of Ezra Pound to James Joyce, with Pound's Essays on Joyce*, ed. Forrest Read (New York, New Directions, 1967), p. 131.

15 *From Critical Writings of James Joyce*, ed. Ellsworth Mason and Richard Ellmann (New York, Viking Press, 1959), p. 243. Note that Joyce strongly identifies himself with the bottom half in his satirical poems, both in this 'gas' from an irritated author and in 'The Holy Office', where the 'office' the author performs for his fellow authors is excretory and cloacal.

16 I owe the literal translation of this phrase to an article in *A Wake Newslitter* which I am unable to locate.

17 Of course, these names are derived from the Prophecies of Malachi.

18 *FW* 170.25, 170.25, 170.26, 171.12, 171.20, 171.29, 172.28, 173.5, 173.20, 174.36, 177.8, 177.9, 177.17, 178.12, 179.13, 180.32, 184.11, 186.14, 187.17, 191.36, 192.5.

19 'Firewater' is gin, made from fermented mash of corn (maize), malt and rye, and only flavored with juniper berries. 'Firstshot' is 'weak poteen of first distillation' (Roland McHugh, *Annotations to Finnegans Wake* (Baltimore and London, Johns Hopkins University Press, 1980), p. 171).

20 See Richard Ellmann, *James Joyce* (New York, Oxford University Press, 1959), p. 469; for the original source, see Frank Budgen, *James Joyce and the Making of 'Ulysses' and Other Writings* (London, Oxford University Press, 1972), p. 172.

21 Molly Bloom acts out the same rhythm. Her menstruation represents the killing of the suitors, those millions of importunate spermatozoa that Blazes has introduced into her. Once they are out, she consummates her love with the rising sun, as a flower of the mountain.

James Joyce
and
the soul

Worshipper of the Word:
James Joyce and the Trinity

ROBERT BOYLE, SJ

The 'word' that James Joyce worshipped is a trinitarian word. I intend in this paper to meditate on that seemingly obvious statement, and I hope to penetrate more deeply into Joyce's artistic vision. Those glimpses that I have so far perceived as through a glass darkly may not be overly profound, but I am fascinated by one or two, such as the realization that Stephen's 'like the God of the creation' image[1] can be developed to accommodate woman as its prime constituent, and that the trinitarian perceptions of St Augustine provide a basic spring for Joyce's verbal riverrun from *Chamber Music* through *Finnegans Wake*.

I begin almost *in termino* with pages 611–12 of *Finnegans Wake*[2] which set forth the chat of 'Paddrock and bookley'. Somewhere along the line in my experience with this stimulating and mysterious passage, I began to suspect that Patrick was delivering the doctrine of St Augustine on the Trinity. I believe it was 'seemingsuch four three two agreement' (*FW* 612.26) that first provided the clue. As I can now reconstruct my experience, I questioned whether Patrick could at this point reasonably be supposed to speak of the date of his arrival as missionary to Ireland, 432 AD, as some sort of basis for any agreement. Since he is saying these words while waving a shamrock (one of the meanings of 'shammyrag') to illustrate his revelations about the Triune God, it may be possible that at that date Patrick's mind could have been full of Augustine's powerful and massive study of the Trinity, *De Trinitate*, published some ten years previously.

The Christian world, in the western church at least, was profoundly interested in the great Bishop of Hippo's trinitarian doctrine, and traveling theologians fresh from Hippo could well have stopped in at the seminary in Gaul where Patrick, reputedly with some difficulty, was attempting to probe the mysteries of the faith. It is Augustine who most perfectly stresses the 'four three two agreement' in the inner life of the one God:

> as My tappropinquish to Me wipenmeselps gnosegates a handcaughtscheaf of synthetic shammyrag to hims hers, seemingsuch four three twoiagreement cause heart to be might, saving to Balenoarch (he kneeleths), to Great Balenoarch (he kneeleths down) to Greatest Great Balenoarch (he kneeleths down quitesomely), the sound sense sympol in a weedwayed-wold of the firethere the sun in his halo cast. Onmen.
>
> (*FW* 612.24–30)

The formula we seminarians bandied about in our Thomistic studies of the Trinity, based firmly on Augustine's teaching, was 'four relations, three persons, two processions'. (We went on with 'one God, no proof' for completeness, that last phrase capable of stressing the mystery or of expressing either a prudent reserve or a cynical doubt.)

Augustine, using Aristotle's category of relation, expresses that the Father is not absolutely a father, but is a father relative to his son – 'This Son is the radiant reflection of God's glory, and the express image of his nature' (Hebrews 1:3). The Son is not absolutely a son, but is so relative to the Father. These are two relations, the Father to the Son, and the Son to the Father. The Father and Son, in mutual love, as one principle breathe forth the Holy Spirit, who fully expresses that love, and whose proper name thus is Love. These are two more relations, the Father and Son to the Holy Spirit, and the Holy Spirit to the Father and Son. Thus does infinite Being eternally know and love, not in time or space, with no beginning or end, with none of the limitations which human attempts to comprehend the mystery tend to project.

And there are two processions – the procession of the Son from the Father, and the procession of the Holy Spirit from the Father and the Son. The first is properly a generation, since the Father, knowing Himself, generates in that knowing a Word expressive of that knowing, which reflects in total perfection the infinite Being. The mutual love of Father and Word breathes forth the third Person, not a generation (since it does not produce a Word imaging the Father), but more properly a spiration, a breathing forth, which, as it were, binds into unity the Father and the Son.

Something of this rattles through Patrick's mind as he waves his crude shamrock symbol, scarcely a symbol that sound sense would approve of. But Patrick aims merely to stress the metaphysical trinitarian problem involving the numbers three and one for the pagan Irish minds accustomed to dealing with these numbers discretely. James Joyce, like Stephen, learned something of the Augustinian doctrine from his catechism. Later Joyce learned much more of it from his probings into St Thomas (as Father Noon has made clear[3]) and also from his passionate contemplation of Dante's musical words. Behind this thorny expression of the debate between St Patrick and the Druid, one of the earliest passages Joyce wrote as he began to bring forth *FW*, lies Joyce's profoundest development of his 'God of creation' image for the artist, the basis of his own adoration of the Word and of his celebration of divine, life-giving women.

Other Augustinian influences appear in Patrick's argument. With his 'shammyrag', his handkerchief of synthetic shamrocks, a nosegay of a sort, Patrick wipes not his nose only but his 'gnosegates'. Here is the voice of Augustine, speaking as he often did of the 'perfect gnosis' which the Manicheans promised him, the key to perfect knowledge. He quested, like some of the fervent young Joyceans committed to psychoanalytic 'principles', for holy certitude. It took him nine years or so of efforts and disillusionments to wipe clear that illusion, and to transcend through Pauline vision the limits of self to the apprehension of God's totally mysterious inner life. This, as I forge Joyce's text in the smithy of my soul (or my imagination), caused Augustine's heart rather than his brain, his will rather than his intellect, to have greater might in his pursuit of truth. Faith, achieved through the activity of the will thrusting beyond the limits of human reason, revealed to Augustine some marvelous insights about the inner life of God. That same faith, which Patrick attempts to preach, uses in Patrick's case the symbolism of the rainbow, as Dante would also do some centuries later.[4]

The Druid, on pp. 611–12, has been concerned with a

Berkeleyan approach to reality through the senses, in this case the eyes dealing with the colors of the rainbow:

> Bymeby, bullocky vampas tappany bobs topside joss pidgin fella Balkelly, archdruid of islish chinchinjoss in the his heptachromatic sevenhued septicoloured roranyellgreenlindigan mantle finish he show . . . zoantholitic furniture, from mineral through vegetal to animal, not appear to full up together fallen man than under but one photoreflection of the several iridals gradationes of solar light, that one which that part of it . . . had shown itself . . . unable to absorbere, whereas for numpa one puraduxed seer in seventh degree of wisdom of Entis-Onton he savvy inside true inwardness of reality, the Ding hvad in idself id est, all objects . . . allside showed themselves in trues coloribus resplendent with sextuple gloria of light actually retained, untisintus, inside them.
>
> (FW 611.4–24)

The best I can make out from this significantly obscure passage is that the Druid, knowing by Druidic science (or perhaps from prophetic insight into modern physics) that the eye can see that one color which the object seen is unable to absorb, draws an apparently obvious conclusion. (The phrase 'fallen man' may be a mixing in of Catholic Patrick's view, or it may be part of the Druid's mythology, or it may be both.) The Druid concludes, as Matthew Arnold would also do some centuries later, that the Kantian aim of seeing the thing as in itself it is can be achieved only inside the human intellect, interpreting on a metaphysical base the misleading evidence of the senses – in this case the sense of vision. The metaphysics appear in 'Entis-Onton', 'being' in Latin and in Greek. The Druid, like Bishop Berkeley later (in the popular view of his philosophy, at least, which Stephen in 'Proteus' seems to expound), enters into his mind (as Berkeley does into his shovel hat on U 48) in order not to *see* but to *think* not only 'distance' but also 'being', quite independently of any Aristotelian matter. Thus the Druid can know King Leary not as he appears but as he really *is* in himself, the very *thing* – green through and through, with the 'viritude' seen only by the sage and without the red-haired 'eruberuption' to be preached a few lines later (FW 612.23) by the saint – neither sage nor saint going beyond probability, one notes. This fluctuation between the possible and the probable, with no certitude in sight, may be an echo of Joyce's very early dealings with this passage in a letter to Miss Weaver, 2 August 1923: 'a piece describing the conversion of S. Patrick by Ireland' (*Letters*, III. 79). The learned Druid, I must say, makes me sympathetic to poor dull-witted Patrick, clumsy even armed as he is with Augustine's learned treatise. Like Patrick, I struggle to probe the Druid's language (which is broken into bits like colors on Berkeley's veil of space scattered on the retina of the eye: 'veil of space with coloured emblems hatched on its field' (*U* 48)); I 'no catch all that preachybook' (*FW* 611.25) either!

The Druid seems to me much like Stephen Dedalus in 'Scylla and Charybdis'. There Stephen, as Father Noon so brilliantly demonstrates in his chapter on 'Sabellian Subtleties',[5] is using the Sabellian position on the Trinity to establish his own subjective, shovel-hat approach to Shakespeare. Falsely based though his position is, as Stephen himself shows that he knows, it does nevertheless serve to probe some fascinating literary problems. Like Joyce, Stephen takes a profound interest in the Trinity for the light it may throw on the position of the artist.

Sabellius, finding the orthodox position of the Trinity incomprehensible, simplified the matter in a way similar to the popular understanding of Berkeley's dealing with color.[6] Sabellius put the solution inside the human head. We think we *see* God as trinitarian, claimed Sabellius, not at all because He *is* that way, 'the Ding hvad in idself id est', but because His operation falls into three modes of being in our process of conceiving Him. The simplicity and completeness of this Sabellian 'solution' proved most attractive to many puzzled Christians. So to those Shakespeare critics (like George Brandes, Frank Harris, Sidney Lee) from whom Stephen drew ammunition for his argument, the treatment of Shakespeare on the basis of the way he operated inside the critics' opinionated heads seemed to them the best way to deal with him. Stephen, as he manipulates the evidence (as with the 'firedrake') to fit his theory, knows he is not dealing with any reality outside himself, but he wants to see how far along he can get with this Sabellian approach. Sabellius destroys the Trinity in fitting it to his limited understanding, as Stephen, in his apparent certitudes about Shakespeare's motives and aims, limits and deforms Shakespeare's works. The ultimate effect is to eliminate mystery. It eases the stress that mystery puts upon human questioning, but, as I see it, ultimately it leaves one paddling in a stagnant subjective morass.

The descent into the self is essential, as both Augustine and Oscar Wilde taught; they also teach that one can't stay there, if one wishes to apprehend the real. Oscar Wilde, in those splendid essays that Mr Best recommended – 'like the Platonic dialogues Wilde wrote' (*U* 214) – takes Matthew Arnold to task for supposing that he has reached what the Druid similarly claims, 'he savvy inside true inwardness of reality, the Ding hvad in idself id est' (*FW* 611.20–1). In this treatment both Kant and Freud are brought to bear on a large Sabellian illusion, that the 'thing' can achieve the divine name 'est' – 'Qui est' or 'He who is' – inside the human head. There the 'est', existence, is that of the owner of the head, and that alone. You have to go into the self, indeed, Augustine perceived, but the next necessity is to thrust beyond the self, to transcend by faith the personal limits: 'He is cured by faith who is sick of fate' (*FW* 482.30–1).

Oscar Wilde put this clearly enough: 'the primary aim of the critic is to see the object as in itself it really is not'.[7] Here Wilde, through his character Gilbert, is putting forth the necessity the artist has to descend into his self and to see things as they are there. When you see an object as it existed in Shakespeare's imagination, you do not see a forest as in itself it is, but as it is transformed by Shakespeare's imagination, given a new being that it can never have in itself. Wilde does not, like Sabellius, suppose that you will see in Shakespeare's imagination – which is to say, in your own imagining of Shakespeare's imagination – any reality that exceeds the actuality of Shakespeare, or of yourself. The Druid supposed that because he could find the sextuple glory of an object's colors in himself (that is, the six colors that the object absorbed) he therefore knew that object as it really is. His construct, like that of phenomenologists in general, is faulty; he does not even consider that the colors inside the object may not be 'colors' at all any more – if indeed they were ever 'colors' outside the human eyeball. Patrick, for all his pragmatic dullness, goes at it the right way. He sees that you must find something from outside yourself, as for example God's revelation of the Trinity, if you are ever to have a chance to apprehend (comprehension is not naturally possible) the being of God. Wilde, dealing with human

art which seeks to express the human experience of a self, still
does not fall into Matthew Arnold's trap of supposing that the
beauty experienced in the self will be the touchstone for an
objective judgment.

Joyce's Druid does fall into Matthew Arnold's trap (which
Stephen's Sabellian theory toys with), and thinks he has trans-
cended the limits of the senses and through intellectual operation
reached certainty and a vision of King Leary. He 'sees' Leary's red
hair as green, and can offer too a true vision of Lord Joss, 'God'
in pidgin English.

Patrick takes up his color approach (and harks back to the first
page of FW, 'and rory end to the regginbrow was to be seen
ringsome on the aquaface' (FW 13–14)). The rainbow, God's
symbol of peace with man, reveals the totality of color, and
suggests that the Druid's science, in resting in the senses' failure
to deal with all seven, fails to reach eschatological reality. Since
we are in time, time limits our approach to the timeless. I spell out
the sentence on FW 612.21–4 somewhat as follows: '(for be-
ingtime [our being is in time] monkblinkers timeblinged [monks
like the Druid and Sabellius and Bishop Berkeley blink and are
time-blinded] complementarily murkblankered [and as well are
blanketed by murk, made murky by too much whiteness of light,
since they get hung up on the distinctions of colors within white]
in their neutrolysis between the possible viritude of the sager and
the probable eruberuption of the saint [they are frustrated
between the possible and the probable and never can actually
reach that subjective certitude which, within the human head, is
the only possible goal]).'

Patrick first waves the symbol of the shamrock – a pitiful
symbol for the relativity of relations which the true apprehension
of God involves: 'as My tappropinquish to Me wipenmeselps
gnosegates a handcaughtscheaf of synthetic shammyrag to hims
hers, seemingsuch four three two agreement cause heart to be
might' (FW 612.24–6). Patrick wants to show that God is both one
and three. His shamrock would better serve the gnostics,
impatient of mystery, than it could illustrate Augustine's doctrine. It is one plant, and it has three leaves. Those leaves are not
the whole plant. Each leaf exists apart from the other two leaves.
They exist absolutely, not relative to each other. Thus they are
synthetic shams, 'synthetic shammyrag', serving better to deny

what Patrick wants to assert than to illuminate it. 'Shamrock' becomes shammyrag, I speculate, from some such mixture as the Irish pronunciation which stresses the guttural aspect of 'k', Shaun's 'shammy mailsack' (*FW* 206.10), a handkerchief in this context, and maybe even the female panties involved in 'shamewaugh' of *FW* 465.8, which Joyce explained to Miss Weaver in a letter of 8 August 1928 as 'sounds also shamrock but means a cloudscreen or shamscreen' (*Letters*, I. 264). ('To hims hers' might be some reflection of Patrick's universal message to men and women. I would like to find in it what I do think I see in Joyce's Trinity, a mingling of human sexes. But here my mind suffers complete neutrolysis.)

More fortunate is Patrick's employment of the rainbow – or, rather, three rainbows, as in Dante's climactic vision:

> saving to Balenoarch (he kneeleths), to Great Balenoarch (he kneeleths down) to Greatest Great Balenoarch (he kneeleths down quitesomely), the sound sense sympol in a weedwayed-wold of the firethere the sun in his halo cast. Onmen.
>
> (*FW* 612.26–30)

An Italian word for 'rainbow', 'arcobaleno', suffers a bit of reversal (milder than the extreme breaking up of the words in parentheses in the Druid's discourse in their effort to enter into his ruthless fracturing of reality) and becomes a name for the trinitarian God showing forth all colors as a symbol of peace between God and man (Genesis 9). 'Arco' is simply 'arch', but 'baleno' offers interesting complexities. The Italian word means 'a flash of lightning', sometimes a continuous flashing, and expresses the effect Hopkins aimed at in his image for the Holy Ghost in 'God's Grandeur': 'It will flame out, like shining from shook foil', meaning, as Hopkins explained to Bridges, the flashes of light from gold foil shaken in the sunlight. In an earlier draft, Hopkins wrote 'like lightning from shook foil', which would be expressed in Italian by 'baleno'. Dante's use of the word indicates a further refinement closer to the 'halo cast' in the quotation from *FW*:

> Mentr' io diceva, dentro al vivo seno
> di quello incendio tremolava un lampo
> sùbito e spesso a guisa di baleno. (*Paradiso*, XXV. 79–81)

> While I was speaking, within the living bosom
> of that fire trembled a flash,
> sudden and frequent, like lightning.

Here 'baleno' expresses the divine fire of love, shining in this case in the bosom of St James. It prepares for the full vision of 'suo fulgore' of Primal Love (*Paradiso*, XXXII. 144).

When the reversed word in *FW* is looked at as an English word, it becomes for me a linkage of 'bale', 'no' and 'arch'. Here I see 'bale' first in its basic Anglo-Saxon and much used sense (cf. the first entry in the *Oxford English Dictionary*) of the evil that destroys that peace between God and man which the rainbow signifies (Genesis 9:13–17). This new divine name for the Persons of the Trinity signifies, as I see it, a denial of 'bale', and expresses the arch that says 'no' to separation between God and man. In its meaning as 'fire', 'bale' expresses pentecostal flame as well as the sunbeams that breathe forth the rainbow. Thus this peaceful fire whose seven colors shimmer in the sevenfold glory of divine life in the Church (conveyed by the seven sacraments, the gifts of the Holy Ghost) offers to the senses of humans a sounder symbol, more objective than the subjective 'sextuple gloria' of the Druid. Here the senses arrive at an objective symbol for the unity of the Father and the Son and the Holy Ghost – a rainbow symbol formed outside the human head by the fire together with the sun casting its halo prismatically through drops of water. That 'halo cast' into the arch of peace well symbolizes the Holy Ghost as well as the holocaust of the total sacrifice, and its shining through so many drops expresses the epiphanic plurality associated with the Spirit, who on the first Epiphany shone 'on men' in the form of tongues of fire.

We have *now* arrived at the unity of 'thing', as the final lines of p. 612 stress:

> That was thing, bygotter, the thing, bogcotton, the very thing, begad! Even to uptoputty Bilkilly-Belkelly-Balkally. Who was for shouting down the shatton on the lamp of Jeeshees. Sweating on to stonker and throw his seven. As he shuck his thumping fore features apt the hoyhop of His Ards.
> Thud.   (*FW* 612.31–6)

In fact, the Druid's 'Ding hvad in idself id est' becomes 'thing', 'the thing', 'the very thing', triply. And the first is the Begetter (the Father), the second the Begotten (the Son), and the third the divine Spirit, silent but veritably and emphatically God; 'begad' suggests a familiar biblical 'begat' as descriptive of the Spirit's relation to the mutual loving spiration of the Father and the Son, 'Father, Word and Holy Breath' (*U* 185) – 'bygotter', 'bogcotton', 'begad!' Those terms lay a basis for recalling Augustine's famous analogy between the inner life of God and the spiritual operations in humans through memory, intellect and will, an analogy also suggested in this text by what happens to the Druid. With his vowels triply doubled and his personality expressed in three separate spiritual operations, reflecting the divine Persons, he is molded like verbal clay into the trinity of 'Bilkilly-Belkelly-Balkally'. The 'Jeeshees' may have some connection with the 'hims hers' a few lines above, but it echoes for me also the Christmas celebration from the root of Jesse at *FW* 502.7–8, 'jusse as they rose and sprungen?'[8] With my own impression of the lamplight on Molly's windowblind as a symbol of the Holy Spirit, which I will discuss at length later, I am tempted to see in this 'lamp of Jeeshees' not only Jesse and his descendant Jesus, God incarnate as the light of the world, but the oil-fed flame of the Spirit as feminine, even plurally a 'she'. The Druid, indeed, seems not to care for the Incarnation, which, as we shall see with Joyce as with Augustine, is the necessary light by which to apprehend the trinitarian vision. I suspect that the Druid's 'stonker' is associated with 'stone', and 'throwing his seven' not only an opposition to Patrick's invocation of the rainbows but maybe also an echo of the dice of the Roman soldiers on Calvary.

The top of p. 613 indicates, I take it, the celebration of Patrick's lighting the Paschal Fire celebrated on Holy Saturday, a liturgy Joyce seldom missed:

> Good safe firelamp! hailed the heliots. Goldselforelump! Halled they. Awed. Where thereon the skyfold high, trampatrampa-tramp. Adie. Per ye comdoom doominoom noonstroom. Yea-some priestomes. Fullyhum toowhom.   (*FW* 613.1–4)

The 'felix culpa', 'o happy sin', attributed to Augustine and a constant echo throughout *FW*, finds expression in the Holy Saturday liturgy when the deacon chants the magnificent 'Exultet'. In Joyce's text the 'sound sense sympol in a weedwayedwold' is emphasized in 'Good safe firelamp'. And the 'heliots', like the 'holytroopers' of the Mime chapter, *FW* 223.11, turning in heliotropic fashion to the sun, echo the lump of gold, 'celestial from principalest of Iro's Irismans ruinboon pot' (*FW* 612.20), the pot at the end of the rainbow. And they chant the liturgical ending to many Catholic prayers, 'Per eundem Dominum nostrum, Jesum Christum, Filium tuum.' Augustine dwells on the 'per', since only *through* the Word-made-flesh can a human approach the mystery of the Trinity.

The ham and eggs a few lines below remind us of the breakfast soon to be served in this resurrection chapter – 'little eggons, youlk and meelk, in a farbiger pancosmos. With a hottyhammyum all round' – and the rainbow's bringing of peace is echoed in 'Gudstruce!' (*FW* 613.11–12).

And yet, has anything happened? 'Yet is no body present here which was not there before. Only is order othered. Nought is nulled. Fuitfiat!' (*FW* 613.13–14). It doesn't look like it, as we take a body count. It looks as if only the order of people (and of words) has changed. That creative 'Fiatfuit' ('Let it be, it was') of *FW* 17.32 gets a different order here, 'Fuitfiat'. Both quite different from that frightening destructive Deity of *FW* 80.24 ff., who deconstructs with his 'As it was let it be', and brings back chaos with his 'rude word'.

But when we can look at this later text in the light of the divine Word, we can perceive that something has happened. The frequent appearance of the opening of John's Gospel, 'In the beginning was the Word', like the opening page of *Ulysses* and the Incarnation imagery introducing Stephen's villanelle, stresses that the divine Word makes a difference. The very sources of creation are stressed on p. 378 in the joining of 'void' and 'word': 'In the buginning is the woid, in the muddle the sounddance and thereinofter you're in the unbewised again, vund vulsyvolsy' (*FW* 378.29–31). Something does at least begin and cease here, so there is more than a mere shifting of order. Some force *not* in the void (in John's Gospel that creative force is the Word) at least has to start the world ('mundus') on its pulsating revolving – though a metaphysician will wonder how those cycling *beings* appear in the void. Precisely what happens cannot be determined from these words, since these plastic words do not exclude contraries. The 'woid' may have the absence of wisdom which 'void' seems to imply, or it may have the fullness of creative wisdom which John's 'Word' explicitly sets forth. Possibly here it has a mixture of both. The fact that it is here a 'buginning' suggests that a bug, perhaps an earwigger, is having an inning – perhaps it found room at the inn.

In the middle things are in a muddle, but sound has begun to operate and dances here in human words. This sound seeks ultimates, one might gather from *FW* 482.33–4: 'That's the point of eschatology our book of kills reaches for now in soandso many counterpoint words.' The Book of Kells reaches for the mystery of the Word-made-flesh and for the still point of the turning wheel – in which stillness the trinitarian dance of knowledge and love circumincesses infinitely. For us in *FW* the muddle bounces us endlessly through an everchanging kaleidoscope of tantalizing beauty. Afterwards and often we find ourselves back in the mystery of the cycling void again. But something has happened.

In *FW* 486.1–2 we find the numbers I take to be the signal more for Augustine than for Patrick alone: 'Are you roman cawthrick 432?' At this point in the chapter, the Four are beginning to probe deeply into Yawn in their psychoanalyzing efforts, deep enough to tap the analogy Augustine finds between human cognitive and volitional stages and the inner life of God. The answer to that question emerges from levels deeper than the Masonic and the Egyptian; it emerges from Augustine's insight, and foreshadows 'such four three two agreement' as we have already seen on p. 612. Here on p. 486 the '432' signals Patrick as conveyer of the Augustinian word, and he is 'cawthrick' perhaps because the Catholic 'coo' of the peaceful Holy Ghost, under the influence of the 'pia et pura bella' of Vico later on this page, changes into the sinister 'caw' of a corpse-loving raven. When Stephen asks, in *Ulysses* 595, 'Where's the third person of the Blessed Trinity' he looks not for a dove but for 'The reverend Carrion Crow'.

That '432' in the opening question triggers a triple riddling answer:

—*Quadrigue my yoke.*
Triple my tryst.
Tandem my sire.   (*FW* 486.3–5)

The answer comes from Yawn, no doubt, and no doubt Yawn with 'three men in him' (*FW* 113.14). He speaks, as I hear him, as one made in the image and likeness of God. If God were answering, the 'my' in the answers could be attributed to the Father in the first case, speaking of the four relations which (as it were) bind the three Persons into unity. In the second case it could be the Son, conceived as between the other two Persons, as in Dante's final trinitarian vision, expressing their triple tryst of infinite love. In the third answer, only the Holy Spirit could be the speaker, since the Father and Son 'sire' him (or her) as one principle. The Holy Spirit could equally well be the speaker of the 'my' in all three cases – we shall later encounter the interesting (inter-EST-ing) word 'mememormee' (FW 628.14).

The examiner, like the 'liplove' in l. 22 below, 'feels' the mouths of the dragoman (the interpreter, the targum-man) openly speaking of the thrills and joys of love (like the young Joyce of *Chamber Music* or the old Joyce celebrating ALP). The infinite triple tryst of lovers is, I take it, being echoed in the human personality of Yawn. That 'overtspeaking' reaches over natural powers, apparently. And the reason appears in 'Plunger words what paddle verbed' (FW 486.9). As Augustine expresses it, after the descent into self the human knower must take the plunge of faith, must transcend the limits of human reason to an intuition of ultimate mystery. Otherwise the human knower will paddle endlessly in the limited and abstract verbiage of popular science and superstition. The indefinite article, 'a', the sign of lack of limitation and thus of abstraction, will be more favored by such a 'knower' than will the definite article, 'the', the sign of that limitation which existing creatures must have. But, with the plunge, wonderful things may happen. We may find ourselves mirroring the infinite ecstasy of love.

The reflection in the mirror is not the 'thing' itself, obviously. But the plunger knows how to word the situation: 'Mere man's mime: God has jest' (FW 486.9–10). This, as I hear it, is the 'mime' that Augustine develops, the human imitation of the Trinity in memory, understanding and will. Memory contains our experience, understanding or intellect words it, and will loves it. Thus, though mere humans, we mime God's infinite life. We reflect divinity.

'God has jest.' The Creator may be enjoying the human comedy, an inept production in the opinion of Stephen as he compares God to Shakespeare: 'The playwright who wrote the folio of this world and wrote it badly' (*U* 213). Or 'jest' may suggest Gloucester's anguished cry, 'As flies to wanton boys are we to the gods' (*King Lear*, IV. i. 38). Or it might echo Pope's polished and balanced nouns, 'The glory, jest, and riddle of the world' (*An Essay on Man*, II). It may suggest God's exploit ('gest') or his epic production, material for Milton.

The 'old order changeth' (*FW* 486.10) enters time once more, returning to the cyclic othering and timely shiftings of the last and the first. The Chinese and Japanese orderings are ancient and shifting in the east as Europe's are in the west, as the 'slingslang' language, sounding whenever eastern myths and doctrines surface, suggests.

The T-square in its Catholic implications I discussed in *James Joyce's Pauline Vision*, pp. 21–2. Joyce uses an ancient and universal liturgical gesture honoring the Trinity, when Catholics, at the Gospel of the Mass, trace a cross on forehead, lips and breast (like Buck Mulligan as the priest scrambles past him, *U* 22). The sign on the forehead honors the source of all being, the Father, the source and seat ('cathedral') of the Word ('brainpan') and of the Spirit ('lovejelly'). He is like 'somebodies', not only consubstantially like the two other Persons of the Trinity, but like all the human somebodies he has created.

He is indeed 'a pious person', the basis of all piety in the old Roman sense of the word, as in 'pious Eneas' of *FW* 185.27. But some background for the 'sound of tistress' which 'isoles the ear' and carries the analyst from the forehead to the lips may be found in *FW* 394.33 ff., where 'that which Itself is Itself Alone (hear, O hear, Caller Errin!)' exteriorizes on this 'ourherenow plane' to share 'passionpanting pugnoplangent intuitions of reunited selfdom (murky whey, abstrew adim!) in the higherdimissional selfless Allself'. Here the God of Jews, Christians and Moslems mixes a bit with the God of the Greeks, and takes some share in the passion of Tristan and Isolde, the lovers of that chapter.

And here we descend from brain through ear, to lips (area of the Word), where feeling predominates, and music ('O la la!') expresses the beauty of the fair lady, a Mercedes or Lady of Shalott, maybe an Irish enchantress like Isolde, source of plenty of distress – she would better fit the phallic suggestion of 'serpe with ramshead'. But to a Catholic imagination (to mine, anyway) this 'serpe' in the context of the Word recalls the serpent Moses raised in the desert (Numbers 21:9) which in John's Gospel signifies Christ on the cross, the extremity of love that lays down its life for its friend. Perhaps here it also suggests the 'penisolate' pen of the artist, 'layed' lightly to the trembling lip. This word speaks of a goddess ('isisglass'); the full expression of this word will occur on the final pages of *FW*.

Joyce through all his work aims at the glorification of woman – really, as I see it, at her deification. The woman of *Chamber Music*, strikingly so in Joyce's arrangement of the poems, centers in the woman of the Canticle of Canticles, the dove. In Joyce's arrangement (the one we have is Stanislaus's), the exactly central poem was the one now numbered 14 (in Joyce's arrangement of 34 poems it was no. 17):

> My dove, my beautiful one,
> Arise, arise! . . .
> My sister, my love,
> White breast of the dove . . .
> My fair one, my fair dove,
> Arise, arise!

That image of the dove, the constant and almost the sole image of the Holy Spirit (except for the flame symbolizing the pentecostal word and the flame of love in the heart), shows up in all Joyce's climactic celebrations of woman, in the wading girl of *Portrait*, in Molly as Dantean Holy Spirit (the dove metamorphosed a bit into roc and auk), and indirectly at least in the dying ALP, sinking like another Leda or the Blessed Virgin of *Portrait*, in the villanelle preparation, under 'whitespread wings . . . come from Ark-angels' (*FW* 628.10).

The 'purity' is qualified both by the ambiguity of 'pura' as an adjective for war, and by the appearance of a favorite trinity, Swift and Stella and Vanessa, 'sey but swift and still a vain essaying' (*FW* 486.26–7). 'Trothed' and 'trenned', I suppose, spring from a doubling and a trining, and this maybe implies some likeness between Swift's problems managing his two girls and the various trinitarian heresies of such interest to Stephen in *Ulysses*, implying similar problems in the divine processions.

Now the final turn of the T-square placed on the breast appeals to the hearing, 'What do you hear, breastplate?' Patrick's poem, 'Breastplate', celebrates the Trinity – 'I believe the Trinity in the

Unity, the Creator of the Universe' – and Yawn concentrating on his breastplate hears a hopper (no doubt the Gracehoper himself) hiding behind the door slapping his feet in a pool of bran – a homely image for the heart's dealing with blood. From the cathedral of the Viconian divine age through the Tennysonian fine lady of the heroic age we come to the basic activities of the human age.

On p. 487 Yawn arrives at a Pauline realization beautifully worded by Hopkins in his 'That Nature is a Heraclitean Fire and of the Comfort of the Resurrection', a poem quoted in *FW* 594.16–17. Yawn states 'and I swear my gots how that I'm not meself at all' (*FW* 487.17–18), and goes on to state that he is going to become something different, something becoming. He speaks, says his examiner, with the voice of jokeup (surely Joyce himself), as a 'craythur', and therefore in attempting to become the Word he will end up being weird (so I gloss) – 'In the becoming was the weared, wontnat!' That 'was' may indicate that time may be the cause of the change in 'word', perhaps combining 'weary' and 'weird'. Hopkins, faced with a realization similar to the one I seem to perceive here in this Augustinian context, indicated that he enters the Godhead (the 'I am') through Christ the divine Word: 'I am all at once what he is, since he was what I am' ('That Nature is a Heraclitean Fire and of the Comfort of the Resurrection').

In knowing the Word we know the Father that the Word perfectly reflects, as Christ pointed out to his followers. It seems to me possible that we may see Stephen in *Portrait* attempting to become the Word, in his villanelle, before he has even tried to plunge beyond self and to seek the Father through the Word. The villanelle is a perfectly appropriate poem to emerge from young Stephen, but it is a thoroughly perverse and rotten poem in itself (if one may so speak of a poem's 'self'). Perhaps it is here that Stephen rejects the plunge of faith, that he paddles and verbs in the stagnant pool of a selfish and defensive self, and that nothing will save him except an adoration of the Word, a successful loving search for the Father and, through the Father plus himself, an unselfish loving vision of the Holy Spirit. For me, Stephen does, at least indirectly, see the Holy Spirit.

Through the revelation of the divine Word, Christ's church through the first four centuries of its existence probed the problems surrounding the mystery of the Trinity.[9] Joyce took passionate interest in that long road to Augustine's own vision, investigating and testing, especially in his development of Stephen, the notable attacks on the Catholic doctrine. I expect that one source of Joyce's interest was his own middle name, which in his pleasantly superstitious way he was surely bound to take as a sign directing him – like the 'unlucky number' (*FW* 307, footnote 7) which refers to Romans 13:13, the passage Augustine read when the voice called to him, 'Tolle, lege', and which, as he describes in his *Confessions*, changed his life – to something like Stephen's winged flight in the wake of Dante, the artist who perfectly expressed Augustine's celestial vision. I think that if we together take a few minutes to consider Joyce's echoes of Dante, we shall see more deeply how Joyce sought, in his great women characters, to express something equal to Dante's vision of the Trinity.

Little Stephen, on the opening pages of *Portrait*, owing to a word mix-up in his head, constructed in his imagination a green rose. Some time later, possibly three or four years, he realizes that he is not likely to find in the less plastic reality outside his head a green rose. Yet he is reluctant to give up his own creation, and thinks that stranger things than finding a green rose have happened. He keeps doggedly searching, and finally, at the end of the fourth chapter, he finds his wild green Irish rose. Like the Druid, he finds a way of perceiving the green where he wants it to be, a bit more objectively. Like Dante, he sees his rose in an ecstatic, supra-rational vision.

The path to that vision is structured on many experiences with women, in a special way with those involving the Madonna and the whore. Stephen deals with both of those (as with all things important to him) in religious contexts, foreshadowing Joyce's own elaborate usage of white and black masses. For my purpose in this paper I shall concentrate on his use of the Blessed Virgin, for him as for Dante an important element in his structuring of the rose.

Stephen falls into extremes of nauseating sentimentality as he oozes his drooling prose expressive of his relationship with the Blessed Virgin. He also involves himself in a material blasphemy (surely not, for him at that age, a formal blasphemy – though in his similar more literary musings in *Ulysses* 242, 'Bawd and butcher', about the heartless Creator of this elaborate cosmic time-machine,

Stephen probably knows well enough what he is doing); he pictures the cruel God as anxious to punish even the appearance of sexual interest in his creatures, while the more understanding and sympathetic mother of Jesus stands between to protect and encourage the young lovers (*P* 116). It is understandable, indeed, how the young Stephen could produce for himself the image of a 'cruel and unfair' pandybatting God; his Madonna construct fits his Clongowes memories of and longings for his own gentle mother. But that sentimental language of the virgin, ironically situated in an echo of Cardinal Newman, whose 'heart to heart' musings on the glories of Mary slide close at times to linguistic goo, does seem to signal an adolescent effort on the part of the still young Joyce to caricature Catholic devotion. Still, it could also be an honest and successful effort to portray the diseased condition of Stephen's own 'Catholic' experience.

In any case, that treatment of the Madonna forms an important stage in Joyce's use of religion for his artistic purposes. It is not pleasant to see Stephen's shy pious murmurs fade into crude perversion and mixture with the guilty joys of whorehouse pleasures:

> If ever he was impelled to cast sin from him and to repent the impulse that moved him was the wish to be her knight. If ever his soul, reentering her dwelling shyly after the frenzy of his body's lust had spent itself, was turned towards her whose emblem is the morning star, *bright and musical, telling of heaven and infusing peace*, it was when her names were murmured softly by lips whereon there still lingered foul and shameful words, the savour itself of a lewd kiss. (*P* 105)

However, it does prepare the reader for Stephen's sharing in Dante's trinitarian vision, indeed for his ultimately going beyond Dante in daring and (maybe) even in achievement. The positive elements in Catholic devotion to the Blessed Virgin, which Dante uses and which Stephen perverts, can fortunately be clearly seen by readers of English in Hopkins's extraordinary 'The Blessed Virgin compared to the Air we Breathe'.[10]

The useful thing to note is that in Catholic devotion, as it developed over the centuries, the Blessed Virgin's role in the church was linked to that of the Holy Spirit. The gradual development of the trinitarian doctrine in the first four centuries of the church, dealing with the central mystery of Catholicism, involved in its own deepening and widening a deeper and wider grasp of everything else in church doctrine. Such development is still going on, since the Catholic Church is still an active society, though for a good deal of Joyce criticism there appears little sensitive awareness of this. For Joyce himself, however, it was an evident fact (as well an unfact), so that his own current language like Dante's can draw nourishment from a living church. He checked out papal encyclicals (including those of Leo XIII, his contemporary), he looked for Vatican reaction to his works, he followed the adventures of Bernard Vaughan, SJ (basis for his Father Purdon), he discussed the Trinity with Budgen, he signed his name as sponsor at the baptism of Ford Madox Ford's daughter (a reluctant godfather talked into a favor for a friend, but he publicly consented to act like a believing Catholic), he lovingly shared experience with his nun-sister in Australia, he kept in yearly touch with favorite liturgies: he knew that Catholic belief, liturgy and language still operate in human affairs.

Mary the mother of Jesus, since she is merely a creature, cannot be a primary source of divine life, but she can be and for Catholics is a necessary channel for divine life. Her act of assent to the proposal of God – 'Behold the handmaid of the Lord. Be it done unto me according to Thy word', words repeated in the Angelus thrice daily in response to the bells that rang at 6, 12 and 6 throughout Joyce's Dublin and which sound throughout *Ulysses* and *Finnegans Wake*, especially in Anna Livia's chapter 8 (8 is also Molly's signifying number) – was for Catholics, as St Thomas beautifully develops, a response of the whole human race, of which God had chosen her as spokesman. As a result, Catholic devotion came to see her role in the activity of divine life (i.e. grace) as accompanying in subordinate fashion the epiphanic and pentecostal activity of the Holy Spirit. As we need God's activity to make us be the Word, we need by God's ordination Mary's assent and cooperation to make us be Jesus, the Word-made-flesh.

Stephen, though on the surface excessively pious, perverts and destroys the Catholic experience in yoking it with his own disordered lustful use, without love, of other human beings, as in his dealings with the young whore at the end of chapter 2 of *Portrait*. His notion of love seems close to that of Joyce in *Chamber Music*, 27:

> Nor have I known a love whose praise
> Our piping poets solemnize,
> Neither a love where may not be
> Ever so little falsity.

Stephen later says he had tried to love God – *trying* to love seems to me analogous to concentrating in order to keep one's blood circulating; love cannot be forced into existence – but Stephen's efforts, as I see them, stem from selfish interest. Love in the Catholic view is the unselfish willing of good to another, not a thing that an animal, a material organism, can naturally do. A spiritual animal, however, responsive and open to its spiritual source, can and will choose to love, unless it chooses to say 'Non serviam!'

Stephen's basic lovelessness (if his complex interior can be so simply categorized) tends to destroy him as a man. As I see it, Stephen's word 'alone' at the close of his theological discussion with Cranly (*P* 147) is closely allied to the 'alone' which hellishly ends James Duffy's literary existence at the end of 'A Painful Case'. However, Stephen's vocation as an artist and his search for the green rose seem to survive and, in the vision of the girl in the water at the close of chapter 4, to flourish.

In this section of *Portrait* Joyce, I believe, constructs his first full-scale effort to echo and equal Dante's music. The girl, a Beatrice figure, seems in Stephen's eyes to have been changed into 'a strange and beautiful seabird'. On her delicate and pure slender leg 'an emerald trail of seaweed had fastened itself as a sign upon the flesh'. (That 'emerald . . . sign', as we shall see, echoes Dante's 'di smeraldo fatte' in *Purgatorio*, XXIX. 125.) She becomes a dove: 'her bosom was as a bird's, soft and slight, slight and soft as the breast of some darkplumaged dove.' Amid the faint noise of the water stirred by her foot, faint as bells, 'a faint flame trembled on her cheek'. The dove and the flame images, with the flame trembling on her cheek, suggest to me the tongues of flame hovering over the heads of the apostles and Mary at Pentecost, and provide a preliminary hint that, like Dante in canto XXXIII of the *Paradiso*, Stephen has seen the Holy Spirit.

Atherton saw the Dantean context of this girl in the water, as he reveals in his note on 'the angel of mortal youth and beauty' (*P* 172): 'The allusions are to Dante's description of a meeting with

Beatrice who represents ideal beauty, at the beginning of *La Vita Nuova*.'[11] Indeed, that 'when she felt the presence and worship of his eyes her eyes turned to his in quiet sufferance of his gaze' (*P* 171) conveys the tone of Dante's attitude toward Beatrice and fairly well translates 'e passando per una via, volse gli occhi verso quella parte ov' io era molto pauroso' (*La Vita Nuova*, III) – 'as she passed by the way, she turned her eyes toward that point where I was filled with fearful wonder' – which foreshadows Beatrice in the heavenly throng some years later, smiling upon Dante:

> Così orai; e quella, sì lontana
> come parea, sorrise e riguardommi;
> poi si tornò a l'etterna fontana.   (*Paradiso*, XXXI. 91–3)

> So did I pray; and she, so distant
> as she seemed, smiled and looked on me,
> then turned again to the eternal fountain.[12]

This passage in *Portrait* of Stephen's vision of the girl in the water sets forth (as *Chamber Music*, which was in a way Joyce's *Vita Nuova*, had foreshadowed) Joyce's early artistic resolve to be not only the new Homer but the new Dante, accomplishing the aim that Dante sets for himself at the end of *La Vita Nuova*: 'spero di dire di lei quello che mai non fu detto d'alcuna' ('I hope to speak of her those words not yet spoken of any woman').

Throughout *Portrait*, Stephen has been searching for a green rose. In 'Aeolus', under the heading of 'Rhymes and Reasons' (*U* 138), which heading implies, for me, how much the music of rhyme, especially trinitarian *terza rima*, in the imagination of a great poet can carry us beyond reason, Stephen recalls three Dantean passages dealing with women. He recalls three rhyming fragments from the speech of the eternally sinful lover Francesca plus her 'per l'aere perso' ('through the murky air') from *Inferno*, V; then three lovely girls in *Purgatorio*; finally the Virgin of *Paradiso*, XXXI, with her golden flame, drawing the fascinated gaze of Dante so that he burned to see yet more. Stephen quotes from the final line of the canto, 'che 'miei di rimirar fé più ardenti' ('that he (Bernard) made mine (my eyes) more ardent in their gazing'), which must surely remind Stephen of his own ardent gazing at the girl in the water some six years previously.

Most significant, however, for my present discussion is

Stephen's recall of the girls in *Purgatorio*, XXIX, 'He saw them three by three, approaching girls, in green, in rose, in russet, entwining' (*U* 138). Dante, experiencing an apocalyptic vision which prepares for the advent of Beatrice, sees the three theological virtues, Charity, Hope and Faith, appearing as three ladies, or gifts ('tre donne'), the first rose-coloured, the second green, the third white:

> Tre donne in giro da la destra rota
> venian danzando; l'una tanto rossa
> ch'a pena fora dentro al foco nota;
> l'altr'era come se le carni e l'ossa
> fossero state di smeraldo fatte;
> la terza parea neve testé mossa.   (121–6)

> three ladies came dancing in a round at the right
>   wheel,
> one of them so ruddy that she would hardly have
>   been
> noted in the fire;
> another was as if her flesh and bones had been of
>   emerald;
> the third seemed new-fallen snow.

Stephen stresses the green girl by mentioning her first, as thoroughly green as the Druid desired to make King Leary be, even to the very bones. The green and the rose engage Stephen's imagination, so that the white of Faith becomes, in Stephen's recall, russet (like the seaweed he had watched swaying in the water, *P* 170), a paler version of the flaming rose of Charity. This recall of Dante's glorious rhymes, so bitter in comparison to the repulsive prose of the old men in the newspaper office (in Stephen's frustrated and vulnerable ear, that is), suggests that the younger Stephen, in his ecstatic linking of the girl in the water to Beatrice, was able to put his Dantean experience to better use.

On 'glimmering and trembling . . . an opening flower' (*P* 172), Atherton notes: 'This seems meant to recall Dante's vision of God as a multifoliate rose (*Paradiso*, Canto 33).'[13] Indeed so! Turning back a few pages of *Portrait* to the preparation for Stephen's Dantean attitude toward the girl in the water, it is easy to spot the reflection of the final cantos of the *Paradiso*. That 'ecstasy of flight' where 'his soul was soaring in an air beyond the world' (*P* 169) made his throat, like Dante's, ache to cry aloud:

> Da quinci innanzi il mio veder fu maggio
> che 'l parlar mostra, ch'a tal vista cede.
> > (*Paradiso*, XXXIII. 55–6)

> Thenceforward my vision was greater
> than speech can show, which fails at such a sight.

Stephen's later search for an augury in the flashing flight of the birds (*P* 224–5) will reflect Dante's image of the message spelled out for him by the flashing lights:

> E come augelli surti di rivera,
> quasi congratulando a lor pasture,
> fanno di sé or tonda or altra schiera.
> > (*Paradiso*, XVIII. 73–5)

> and as birds, risen from the shore,
> as if rejoicing together at their pasture,
> make of themselves now a round flock,
> now some other shape.

And the eagle Stephen desires to imitate (*P* 169) may stem, I believe, from Dante's Johannine eagle outlined in the heavens:

> e quietata ciascuna in suo loco,
> la testa e 'l collo d'un'aguglia vidi
> rappresentare a quel distinto foco.
> > (*Paradiso*, XVIII. 106–8)

> and when each had rested in its place,
> I saw the head and neck of an eagle
> represented by that patterned fire.

And from the 'gross voice of the world of duties and despair' (*P* 169) Stephen heard the 'call of life', as Dante hears the eagle speak of the 'just and duteous' state which leads to the vision of infinite love:

> E quel che mi convien ritrar testeso,
> non portò voce mai, né scrisse incostro,
> né fu per fantasia già mai compreso. . . .
> E cominciò: 'Per esser giusto e pio

son io qui essaltato a quella gloria
che non si lascia vincere a disio . . .'
                              (*Paradiso*, XIX. 7–9, 13–15)

And that which I must now tell,
never did voice report nor ink record,
nor was it ever comprised by phantasy. . . .
And it began, 'For being just and duteous
am I here exalted to that glory
which cannot be surpassed by desire . . .'

Stephen feels that he will see 'strange fields and hills and faces' (*P* 170), and so indeed does Dante:

Poi, come gente stata sotto larve,
che pare altro che prima, se si sveste
la sembianza non süa in che disparve,
cosi mi si cambiaro in maggior feste
li fiori e le faville, sì ch'io vidi
ambo le corti del ciel manifeste.   (*Paradiso*, XXX. 91–6)

Then, as folk who have been under masks
seem other than before,
if they do off the semblances
not their own wherein they were hid,
so into greater festival
the flowers and the sparks did change
before me that I saw both
the courts of Heaven made manifest.

And as Stephen, barefoot like Moses before the burning bush, 'wondered at the endless drift of seaweed' and sees how the water was dark with endless drift and mirrored the high-drifting clouds (*P* 170), so Dante faced with the heavenly Rose seeks to image his vision:

E come clivo in acqua di suo imo
si specchia, quasi per vedersi addorno,
quando è nel verde e ne' fioretti opimo,
sì, soprastando al lume intorno intorno,
vidi specchiarsi in più di mille soglie
quanto di noi là sù fatto ha ritorno.
                              (*Paradiso*, XXX. 109–14)

And as a hillside mirrors itself
in water at its base,
as if to look upon its own adornment
when it is rich in grasses and in flowers,
so above the light round and round about
in more than a thousand tiers
I saw all that of us have won return up there.

And as Stephen drifts off to blissful sleep at the end of chapter 4, the language which closes his vision echoes, to my ear, the tone and rhythm of the *Paradiso*'s sublimely subdued music in its dying fall: 'islanding a féw laŝt fígures in dístant póols' – 'l'amór che móve il sóle è l'áltre stélle'.

In any case, I see that Stephen constructs for this girl a context which in Dante went beyond Beatrice to surround the Blessed Virgin herself – 'figlia del tuo figlio', as Bernard addresses her in the first line of the final canto. This phrase Stephen makes rather nasty use of in his drunken Mass (*U* 391). It becomes likely that the Holy Spirit is not absent from his imagination, even though he goes on to quote phrases from the fairly psychotic Léo Taxil, in an even nastier passage suggesting a Leda-and-the-swan relationship between Mary and 'le sacré pigeon' (*U* 391). I think that Stephen, sobering and having drunk the milk of a goddess, returns to something closer to his *Portrait* ecstasy when a 'visible splendid sign' illumines 'the mystery of an invisible person' (*U* 702) during his final moments of existence in the book. The girl in the water had prepared him to draw Dantean inspiration from the more cosmic goddess of Eccles Street.

In my own vision of Joyce's imagination, that lovely line quoted above, 'sì, soprastando al lume intorno intorno' (*Paradiso*, XXX. 112 – 'so, above the light round and round about'), may be a basis for the 'visible luminous sign' (*U* 702) on Molly's window-blind and for 'an inconstant series of concentric circles' (*U* 736) on Molly's ceiling, in which context, as I see Joyce's vision, Molly takes her place in the trinitarian circles themselves.

The interpretation of Molly as Holy Spirit (a notion that I consider Joyce also held and expressed) at times tends to evoke not only disagreement but even hostility. Some hearers seem to think I want to pervert good healthy dirty-minded Molly to Catholic sanctity. Well, I take Molly as I see her, and, while there is in Molly ignorance and immorality and narrowness, there is also shrewd perceptiveness and kindness and sympathy, talent and drive and frustration, concern for daughter and sorrow for dead son, a complex fondness for her husband, a strong drive for sexual and artistic fulfillment, a hope that things might get better, and a refreshing involvement with life. The whore does operate in Molly, but so does the Madonna. And beyond that, in Catholic eyes at least (mine anyway), Molly has the same goal that every other human being (whether made from flesh or from ink) has – to share the infinite life of the Trinity. I see then in Molly what Augustine would have seen and what, I believe, James Augustine Joyce did see: the capacity to be God. Thus it is not impossible for Molly to represent divine operations in *Ulysses*. Nobody gets excited if Bloom is somehow equated with the Father, if Stephen is seen as what he calls himself, Eternal Son. Why then be upset if Molly is glorified as the Holy Spirit?

One might answer that in Catholic tradition the Holy Spirit is male, so that Joyce would not be likely to see her as the third Person. But that seems to me a most feeble objection. It is true that in prayers the male pronoun is used for the Spirit, but in any case that is simply convention. Sex applied to any Person of the Trinity is obviously an extrinsic attribution made by limited human animals. Convention and revelation agree that Father and Son are terms admirably suited, even with the sexual limitations involved, to human attitudes toward the first and second Persons. There has been a strong movement throughout the centuries, however, to avoid anthropomorphic representations of the third Person as a third male. The use of the dove as a symbol of the Holy Spirit in iconography was formally approved by a local council of Constantinople in 536. Anthropomorphic depiction of the Spirit as a third male declined after the Middle Ages until finally such depiction was declared unacceptable in a decree by Benedict XIV on 1 October 1745. The dove has served, particularly in depictions of the Annunciation to the Blessed Virgin, of the baptism of Christ and of Pentecost (in addition to the tongues of flame). The dove stresses the life-giving, peaceful, devoted activities of the Holy Spirit. The gentle quiet of the dove resembles the quiet of the Spirit, who, though the Inspirer and Author of revelation, never directly speaks.

The result has been that it is easy to treat the Spirit as feminine, and it has often been done. In the second verse of Genesis, the Spirit (the Hebrew *ruah* is a feminine noun) broods on the water. There is by no means agreement among Scripture scholars on that translation, but it is the one Joyce grew up with. We see it operating in Hopkins's great sonnet on the Holy Spirit, 'God's Grandeur':

> And the Holy Ghost over the bent world
> Broods with warm breast and with ah! bright wings.

That is a female bird. Its operation of fostering and protecting life is like that of Mary in 'The Blessed Virgin compared to the Air we Breathe'. The Spirit shares the Word with us, one might say, as Mary shares the flesh with us, so that the Word-made-flesh lives among us and in us, if we will accept him. That way of putting it, with its suggestion of equating infinite Being with the finite operation of a creature, is imperfect, but the statement can be understood in a perfectly orthodox way. It may be useful to recall, too, that in Catholic liturgy the Jewish personification of Wisdom as a woman is applied both to the Holy Spirit and to Mary.

Joyce at any rate seemed to find no difficulty in judging that a woman can far better represent the Spirit than could any male. As I see the text of *Ulysses*, it presents Molly to us as Holy Spirit quite as clearly as it presents Bloom as Father and Stephen as Eternal Son. I see sufficient Dantean clues to convince me.

In 'Ithaca' the preparations for another Dantean trinitarian vision begins, as I see it, with the wanderings among the constellations. The celestial spectacle confronting Bloom and Stephen as they liturgically emerge from the lower depths 'into the penumbra of the garden' (*U* 698) clearly relates, as a number of critics have noted, to the closing lines of Dante's *Inferno*, XXXIV. 136–9:

> . . . el primo e io secondo,
> tanto chi'i' vidi de le cose belle
> che porta 'l ciel, per un pertugio tondo.
> E quindi uscimmo a riveder le stelle.

> . . . he first and I second,
> so far that through a round opening I saw
> some of the beautiful things that Heaven bears;
> and thence we issued forth to see again the stars.

Bloom and Stephen urinate; in the garden of purgation they both, in concert, purge themselves. Like the Father and Son in the Trinity breathing forth the Spirit of Love as one principle, Bloom and Stephen fix their gaze, in language suitable for a liturgical situation, to a 'visible luminous sign' (*U* 702) where oil furnishes light. 'Oil' is one of the names of the Holy Spirit, 'Et spiritalis unctio' ('and anointing of the spirit') in the ninth-century hymn, 'Veni, Creator Spiritus'. Oil is used in many sacramental operations as a symbol of spiritual light-giving power, of healing and of refreshing, as with the 'sweet ointments' of the bridegroom in the Canticle of Canticles. Hopkins uses both the healing and refreshing aspects in 'God's Grandeur':

> It gathers to a greatness, like the ooze of oil
> Crushed . . .
> And wears man's smudge and shares man's smell.

In this 'visible luminous sign', it seems to me, lies the answer to Stephen's question at *U* 595, 'Where's the third person of the Blessed Trinity?' As these two persons, after their liturgical entrance, contemplate that sign, Bloom elucidates 'the mystery of an invisible person'. Bloom with his good eyes sees 'the projected luminous' and Stephen sees 'semi-luminous shadow', while together they urinate. But before they enter into that human operation they enter in silence into the operation proper to the divine Father and His Son, who is the perfect mirror of the Father. The consubstantial Father and Son contemplate reciprocal Spirit; this human father and son, having together looked at the sign of an invisible person (the son directed to it by the father), were then silent, 'each contemplating the other in both mirrors of the reciprocal flesh of theirhisnothis fellowfaces.' They see each other face to face, not as in a glass darkly. In such a context, could any perceptive reader fail to suspect, at least, that the invisible person denoted by a visible splendid sign is the Holy Spirit, and that the suggestion made by the elucidator is that they join in affection and admiration for that third person?

A celestial sign follows, uniting the three persons: 'A star precipitated with great apparent velocity across the firmament from Vega in the Lyre above the zenith beyond the stargroup of the Tress of Berenice towards the zodiacal sign of Leo' (*U* 703). Thus I see the Word (Stephen the Lyre, the Irish as well as the

Jewish harp) joined with the Father (Leopold) through their common interest in the Spirit of Love (Molly of the fair tresses).

In *Paradiso*, canto XXVII, occurs the passage which, according to the brilliant insight of Richard Ellmann (in *Ulysses on the Liffey*, pp. 171–2), indicates 'why Molly Bloom had to be born so far from Ireland, at the pillars of Hercules', and links with that celestial sign in *Ulysses*. Dante and Beatrice look down on 'the mad track of Ulysses' from Greece to Gibraltar:

> sì ch'io vedea di là da Gade il varco
> folle d'Ulisse, e di qua presso il lito
> nel qual si fece Europa dolce carco.   (82–4)

> so that, on the one hand, beyond Cadiz, I saw
> the mad track of Ulysses, and on the other nearly to
>   the shore
> where Europa made herself a sweet burden.

Europa indeed made herself a sweet burden, and the results gave the Stephen of *Portrait* his Minos, his Pasiphaë, his Minotaur, his maze, his own winged futile flight too close to the sun.

In the lines of *Paradiso* which follow, Dante gazes into the face of Beatrice as (I take it) Stephen gazes with Leopold at the luminous sign of Molly's invisible presence. For Dante

> E la virtù che lo sguardo m'indulse,
> del bel nido di Leda mi divelse
> e nel ciel velocissimo m'impulse.   (97–9)

> And the power which her look granted me
> drew me forth from the fair nest of Leda
> and thrust me into the swiftest of the heavens.

Stephen too is drawn forth from the fair nest of Leda. The fair nest for Dante is in the constellation of Gemini, from which Dante and Beatrice view Gibraltar. The twins, Castor and Pollux, were the children of Leda, who, after Jupiter as a philandering swan had impregnated her, brought forth two eggs, 'from one of which issued Helen, and from the other twin brothers' (Ovid, *Heroides*, xvii. 55–6).[14] Dante goes on to the vision of the Trinity, but Stephen again sets forth on his own, once again winging east. I believe that the omens indicate, unlike Tindall's view that

Stephen strode off to write *Ulysses*, that it is at least equally likely that Stephen may drown this time.

With Poldy, however, we can enter the House of Bondage and find our own paradisaical vision. With Leopold we end, as 'Ithaca' comes to a close, in the nest of Leda. The two eggs are here – or, it appears, one egg from two birds, the large mythical roc and the small real auk, one suitable for Gibraltar, the other for Howth: 'Going to a dark bed there was a square round Sinbad the Sailor's roc's auk's egg in the night of the bed of all the auks of the rocs of Darkinbad the Brightdayler' (*U* 737). The eggs symbolize, I take it, Molly's two natures: her divine nature, as 'Gea-Tellus . . . big with seed' (*U* 737), thus with at least one egg in her (the original Gea, as Earth, the mother of all creatures, must have had many); her human nature, as mother of two.

The most important item, for me, on this page so important to Bloom, is the squaring of the circle. Bloom sees 'a square round Sinbad the Sailor's roc's auk's egg' (*U* 737). (In 'Circe' Virag had sniggered at Bloom's intention 'to devote an entire year to the study of the religious problem and the summer months of 1882 to square the circle and win that million', *U* 514–15.)

As Dante in Paradise gazes enraptured at the center circle, he uses this startling image:

> Qual è 'l geomètra che tutto s'affige
> per misurar lo cerchio, e non ritrova,
> pensando, quel principio ond' elli indige,
> tal era io a quella vista nova . . . (*Paradiso*, XXXIII. 133–6)

> As is the geometer who wholly applies himself
> to measure the circle, and finds not, in pondering,
> the principle of which he is in need,
> such was I at that new sight.

Charles Singleton stresses the power of this extraordinary image:

> No poet was ever so daring in his final simile. . . . But the reader who feels amazement at the geometrical abstractness of the final vision, face to face, should ask himself how *he* would present God to the reader, were he the poet. Would God the Father be an elder with a long grey beard, would the Son appear anthropomorphically as such (as in so many Italian paintings), and would the Holy Ghost be a dove? Would he

have his poem end in such a vision of the Deity? [15]

It is this most striking single image that Joyce chooses, in my view, to carry us to some appreciation of the wonder and reverence of Bloom as he finally achieves the vision he had vainly sought in the museum. There he went to investigate the physical attributes of the goddesses. He even manages to include the Blessed Virgin in his large notion of goddesses: 'By Bassi's blessed virgins Bloom's dark eyes went by. Bluerobed, white under, come to me. God they believe she is, or goddess. Those today I could not see' (U 259). Now in Molly's bed he sees, and, going all the way in acceptance and love, he squares the circle and enters that Joycean Promised Land that Bloom, unlike Moses, could enter. Bloom is gazing upon 'adipose posterior female hemispheres, redolent of milk and honey' (U 734). More daring than Dante, Joyce dares to form an analogy between Molly's buttocks and Dante's symbol of the infinite Trinity. So perfectly and so subtly does he do it, weaving (as Dante does) many complex and unexpected threads into his large epic and making full use of Dante's sublime achievement, that reverently and joyfully we slip with Bloom into the timeless flow of Molly's own circling consciousness, as into a human paradise, a garden of delights where reason must plunge outward into mystery.

This invocation by Joyce of Dante's vision makes it possible, as I see it, to carry the trinitarian suggestions of the 'mystery of an invisible person' (U 702) into a full acceptance of Molly as the Holy Spirit of this book. In Dante's vision the middle circle represents the Son, but Augustine's triangle of relations might better (certainly as well) be represented by the Holy Spirit in the middle, binding the Father and Son into one. Stephen's Sabellian creed (U 197) pictures 'middler the Holy Ghost' between the modes of Begetter and Begotten. And in seeing Molly this way I see another possibility that, if Joyce did not see, I figure he would like and assent to. As Molly herself goes out of existence on her dominant word 'yes', I see her operating in timeless fashion to get this whole book into operation. I see her as the life-giving power who binds this book into a unity. She is not only the necessary countersign for Bloom's visa into eternity, but she is also the force that makes Bloom's and Stephen's worlds become (at least in some respects, at least for a time) one.

Like a great dove brooding on the waters (or on a roc's auk's egg), she concludes her existence brooding on her own loves on Gibraltar and on Howth, conflating them timelessly into one. She can do that because, as I imagine her, she exists on at least three of the four Dantean levels, the literal, the moral, the allegorical and the anagogical.[16] On the literal plane, Molly broods in bed at 7 Eccles Street in the wee hours of 17 June 1904. On the allegorical plane, as earth-goddess she has less limitation from time and place, and can actually operate on Howth with Bloom in May of 1888 and on Gibraltar with Mulvey in May of 1886. On the anagogical plane, where she is the Holy Spirit, divine in the Dantean sense, she enjoys infinite being with no limitations whatever from time and space. Hence, as it were from the spot on Howth where in May of 1888 she looked southward, across the bay, she can simultaneously see Buck Mulligan, on the morning of 16 June 1904, sending papal benedictions her way, and she can respond to his whistle, passing over the Electric Power Plant ('the Pigeon House') as she overshadows his mocking Eucharist like the Power overshadowing Mary at the Incarnation. Buck calls for more 'current' from the Holy Spirit, by whose power the sacraments come into being and operate, to hasten the confection of his burlesque consecration on the opening page of *Ulysses*.

The two answering whistles perhaps come, literally, from swimmers at the 40 Foot who respond to the whistle they hear, but metaphorically and allegorically those three whistles fill out the trinitarian signal proper to the Consecration, formerly sounded out with a little bell by the server at Mass; anagogically, I believe, the whistles signal Molly's divine intervention. As Holy Spirit she does bring a source of inspiration, perhaps to the mockery of Buck as she is herself a mocking Spirit, but as well a possibility of true artistic life to the observing Stephen, who will on the literal level drink her cream at another less mocking Mass conducted by Bloom before another sunrise, will contemplate her picture, establishing some connection with 'the King of Spain's daughter' (*U* 652), and will gaze at the light signaling her presence at the moment of a crucial parting. On the anagogical level, as I see it, it is Molly who gives life to the whole world of *Ulysses*. On at least two of her four levels Molly offers life, through Bloom, to Stephen the potential son and lover. Joyce, unlike his protégé Beckett, had no distaste for anagogy, and I find in the Augustinian, Aquinian and Dantean counterpointing of Molly's varied levels a most delightful and illuminating 'point of eschatology' (*FW* 482.33).

Invigorated by so inspiring a celebration of feminine power, shining with the reflections of circling Dantean rainbows, I turn with anticipation to the magnificent poem, Anna Livia's final soliloquy, which brings *FW* either to a plunge back to the timely riverrun of the Liffey or into the timeless blankness of the white page, now not vacuous but significantly silent, like the blank spaces of Mallarmé's 'Un coup de dés', a silence of the mind.

However, as usual, when I approach *FW* not just with open acceptance but with some goal in mind, I find resistance and frustration. The text never looks the same as it did the last time. Indeed, everything connected with it is 'moving and changing every part of the time' (*FW* 118.22–3). I hear, indeed, the voice of Anna each time, but so many other voices too. And Anna changes. Still, this time I listen and peer, hoping to catch some glimpse of that Dantean glory so evident in the clear vision of the wading girl in the water, less clear but discernible in the circles of Molly's bottom (cf. 'Venus Kallipyge', *U* 201), and sure now to be gleaming forth in this supreme vision of human death and rebirth. But once again I find sullen and silent resistance.

Then my eye falls upon the closing paragraphs of Anna's Letter, and the text begins to come into focus:

> Only look through your leatherbox one day with P.C.Q. about 4.32 or at 8 and 22.5 with the quart of scissions masters and clerk and the bevyhum of Marie Reparatrices for a good allround sympowdhericks purge, full view.   (*FW* 618. 12–15)

4.32! I look about for Patrick and find 'St Patrick's purgatory' two lines below, in full view. I note the period after the 4, but even that does not clue me in. The note in Roland McHugh's *Annotations to Finnegans Wake*[17] alerts me to paying attention to the way I *said* '8 and 22.5', and then I perceive I am dealing with the time on a clock, no doubt an alarmclock, and that eight and twenty to five also expresses 4.32 – approaching time to get up. The St Patrick's purge group, with the pope's wife Lily 'pulling a low' (*FW* 618.17), looks promising but confusing; therefore I sweep on into the soft music of the final soliloquy, and look hard at Sinbad the Sailor (thus I read 'somebalt thet sailder' at *FW*

620.7). I brighten at the echo of St Paul's 1 Corinthians 15:52 expression of the Resurrection 'in the twinngling of an aye' (*FW* 620.14–15). I wonder if the flame to burn the Phoenix, no doubt the rising sun, might be the newborn day triumphantly announced by St Michael in Sterne tones – 'It's Phoenix, dear. And the flame is, hear! Let's our joornee saintomichael make it' (*FW* 621.1–2) – faintly reflecting Dantean light.

The visit to the Old Lord of Howth, who opens the door to a new era and who gives gifts at Easter (*FW* 623.4–9), gives me a passing pulsation of hope. The well-hidden Swiftean context concealing the Augustinian *o felix culpa* holds me for a complex second (*FW* 623.21–4); 'the hardest crux ever' I nod at (*FW* 623.33–4). I hear the angelic salutation and Mary's response, as in the Angelus ('The angel of the Lord declared unto Mary, and she conceived of the Holy Ghost. . . . Behold the handmaid of the Lord, be it done unto me according to thy word'), cleverly involved in that 'hark from the air' from Captain Finsen (the eschatological Lord), which presses the divine suit to the human race, and because of Mary's response we receive the Word through her ear (*FW* 624.27–31). The Vanity Fair of literature and history, including the motto of the Order of St Patrick (as McHugh's *Annotations* reveals), does little to help me (*FW* 625.5–7), and the revelation that Howth has become Mt Olympus (*FW* 625.21) leaves me cool. Anna losing her breath and asking for silence in which to remember (a Beckettian attitude of great interest to me, but not in itself obviously Dantean) holds me briefly (*FW* 625.28–9). The Olympian storms and rainbows hold promise (*FW* 626.15–21), though these Wagnerian horns sound uncompromisingly earthy. The fear of Anna at the 'sheeny stare' of the 'great black shadow' (*FW* 626.24, 25) takes me back to Buck's warning to Stephen (*U* 217) about the stare of black-garbed Bloom the sheeny (*U* 200), which was what the sensual Buck could not fathom, the desire of the father for a son. Joyce himself, according to Mercanton,[18] shivered at the recollection of these thunderbolts. The atmosphere is, in Greek context, impressive, but far from Dante's. Anna sees herself among this wild Wagnerian group of 'stormies' (*FW* 627.31), far from Paradise. The threefold father at the top of the final page raises hope, but his powerful grasp of Neptune's trident keeps things turbulent.

Still, the water (and the music of the words) now begins to calm, with only 'Two more. Onetwo moremens more' to go (*FW* 628.5–6). One leaf remains. It is not only one of those rustling leaves of *FW* 202.31 or the falling leaves of *FW* 619.20–3, but it is this last leaf of this book. It will serve to remind Anna of many aspects of life ('Lff!'), and it reminds me with a great surge of interest of *Paradiso*, XXXIII. 85–7:

> Nel suo profondo vidi che s'interna,
> legato con amore in un volume,
> ciò che per l'universo si squaderna.

> In its depth I saw ingathered, bound by love
> in one single volume, that which is dispersed
> in leaves throughout the universe.

'Squaderna' involves both 'scattered', 'unbound', and 'quaderno', quire of a book. Thus Joyce takes up another striking image from Dante's climactic vision, now suggesting a parallel between the leaves of *FW* and the works of the God of creation, between his words and the Word of God. 'In the beginning was the word', as the previous 627 leaves of this book give testimony. Now this last one clings to Anna, reminding her of her own Penelopean activity in *FW* 28.6–8, 'watching her sewing a dream together, the tailor's daughter, stitch to her last.' Then the lips, now drying, would moisten once again 'As when you drove with her to Findrinny Fair' (*FW* 28.12–13). Finn was the creator then indeed: 'Creator he has created for his creatured ones a creation' (*FW* 29). Triply her father, he is seen by Anna as the Virgin in pictures of the Annunciation saw the dove, or as Noah (or Mrs Noah) saw the dove returning to the Ark of the Covenant (with the rainbow near by), and, awed, she feels a fall threatening her, like the Humpty Dumpty one ('humbly dumbly', *FW* 628.11) which opened this cycling book ('tumptytumtoes' *FW* 3.21).

Anna seems to be sinking in ecstasy, which is what Dante does as he approaches his own vision of the Father:

> Un punto solo m'è maggior letargo
> che venticinque secoli a la 'mpresa
> che fé Nettuno ammirar l'ombra d'Argo.
> (Paradiso, XXXIII. 94–6)

> A single moment makes for me greater oblivion

> that five and twenty centuries have wrought
> upon the enterprise that made Neptune wonder
> at the shadow of the Argo.

Thus the wondering Neptune in Dante's text parallels the wondering, frightened Anna fearing to lose her being in the triple terrible 'prongs' of the Trinity, appearing to her as Neptune. Her fear parallels that of Hopkins at the opening of *The Wreck of the Deutschland*, when he fears to lose his being if he says 'yes' to the looming electric infinite presence who touches his inmost heart.

In the collocation of the two Neptune images, we can observe how Joyce's text begins to move from the Grecian Olympus and the Wagnerian surging sensual music of the previous pages into the Dantean Paradise and the Brucknerian religious sublimity of this final clinging page. Dante's Neptune wonders at the Argo, the first ship ever made, as a comparison for Dante's wonder at his vision of the Word. Joyce's Neptune, a frightening apparition for the triply named father at the top of *FW* 628.1–2, becomes the loving father who bore little Anna through the perils and joys of becoming. She wonders at him now, as an object of worship, 'only to washup' (*FW* 628.11).

Like Molly Bloom (who also ends on the top of Howth), she assents to human limitations of time, 'Yes, tid' ('tid' is Danish for 'time', as the 'Far' who soon calls is 'father' in Danish – Father Ibsen's influence on Joyce, no doubt). And of space, 'There's where' (*FW* 628.12).

'First.' At the waking of life we pass from the quiet womb through the pubic bush to the noisy 'whish' of wind and motion. But there is much more in these whirling cycles than we can observe in our restless motion. There is the still center of the turning wheel, which we can find, especially if with Dante and Joyce we achieve the vision, and it is worded within this remarkable 'whish' itself, seemingly so volatile and noisy. It contains the praise of the 'leafy' Anna in *FW* 619.20, at the beginning of her soliloquy. There she was, on this golden anniversary (as in *FW* 104.9, 'My Golden One and My Selver Wedding'), the 'May . . . goolden' (*FW* 619.30 – a reflection of Stephen's lovely mother, May Goulding) expressing thanks to 'toddy' for boring her (*FW* 619.33). Her 'Yawhawaw' (*FW* 619.34) could be a yawn or a pleased cry – or both, perhaps. One thing it obviously does is to suggest the name of Yahweh, the sacred tetragrammaton.

The ever-helpful Mrs Glasheen has an enlightening note in *A Wake Digest*[19] on the tetragrammaton in *FW*. She finds *FW* 597 crowded with the four consonants: 'IHVH, JHVH, JHWH, YHVH, YHWH, that is, I, J, Y are interchangeable, and so are W, V.' She notes that the last word in *FW* 597.36, 'whish', includes all the letters of the tetragrammaton, as IHWH, and the Greek symbol for Jesus, IHS.

It is with this sacred little word 'whish' that I ended my book, *James Joyce's Pauline Vision*. The central element in Paul's own vision was the mystery of the Trinity, revealed to him through his faith in the mystery of the Incarnation. This vision came to Augustine primarily from Paul, from Augustine to St Thomas Aquinas, from Thomas to Dante, and from Dante to Joyce. This word 'whish', thus, as tetragrammaton and as IHS, expresses the Jewish revelation of the one God, the Christian revelation of the Trinity, and the mystery of the Word-made-flesh. It involves the Father as Creator as the Jews knew God, the Word as Christians know Christ the Son of God, and (in its sound of pentecostal wind) the Holy Spirit. In all these ways I perceive it operating in Anna Livia's expression of the brief passage of human life and the whole swift progress of this book, when both of them are, like Dante's vision

> . . . quasi conflati insieme, per tal modo
> che ciò ch'i' dico è un simplice lume.
>
> (*Paradiso*, XXXIII. 89–90)

> as though fused together in such a way
> that what I tell is but a simple light.

This is like the moment of the kaleidoscope's pause, which Joyce expressed so powerfully in *FW* 143. There, when time and space were shaken together, 'an earsighted view of old hopeinhaven' like Dante's vision could be had 'at this auctual futule preteriting unstant' (*FW* 143.7–8). Everything in what Eliot in 'The Dry Salvages', V, calls 'the moment in and out of time' takes place, like the artist's life story written on his own skin, in 'one continuous present tense' (*FW* 185.36–186.1). The 'actus', past participle of 'agere', to act, ingests 'auctus', past participle of 'augere', to grow, to change, and thus, in 'auctual', expresses an act which extends vertically as well as horizontally, which peers into eternity as it seems to pause in time. 'Future', which has no real existence outside the mind and thus cannot act on its own, combines with 'futile'. 'Preterite', which expresses past time, takes on the form of a present participle, and thus expresses the past acting in the present. 'Instant' loses its static quality and ceases to stand as it thrusts through to eternity and becomes an 'unstant'. Thus all time combines in the one really existing present moment, which, if it can be lifted or expanded outside time and space, will give us an inexpressible glimpse of eternity. It is such a moment at which both Dante and Joyce aim in their efforts to deal in eschatological terms with the ultimate in mysterious human experience. The word 'whish' serves Joyce's purpose well.

Anna's 'End here' fulfills the prophesy of *FW* 28.27–9, 'There'll be bluebells blowing in salty sepulchres the night she signs her final tear. Zee End.' And her 'Finn, again' (*FW* 628.14) wipes out the absolving 'Finn no more' (*FW* 28.34) of that same page. She offers a kiss, and she offers herself, and it is here that my own mind gets carried into the Dantean ecstasy. I see (or think I see) in Anna's 'mememormee' (*FW* 628.14) an expression of trinitarian mystery which fulfills all the promise I saw (or thought I saw) in *FW* 611–12 and 486–7.

The word, first of all, follows in line from 'Remember' in the Letter at *FW* 617.26, from 'You remember?' of *FW* 622.17, from the especially significant 'remember' of *FW* 625.29. But, beyond those, this 'Remember me' inevitably recalls, in the context of Joyce's work, the pitiful cry of a father, the ghost of Hamlet Senior. In 'Circe', as we have seen, Stephen, having fled from the ghost of his mother, ties up under the invocation of St Patrick (a saint also invoked by Hamlet) another cry of Hamlet Senior, 'Hamlet, revenge!' (*U* 595), and turns away from the Irish sentimentality of Old Gummy Granny with what I take to be on Stephen's part a cynical sneer at the elaborate and etherial convolutions of Catholic theology and on Joyce's part a structural expression of profound theological (and Dantean) mystery: 'Where's the third person of the Blessed Trinity?' (*U* 595). For Stephen, I surmise, the answer is, 'Nowhere, except in your soggy, sentimental, and depraved, priestridden imaginations.' For Joyce, I believe the answer is, 'In bed at 7 Eccles Street.'

Anna means her expression in the most positive way, I should judge. She loves and accepts and desires return of love. She might too, as the mother of little Shem, the 'god in the manger' (*FW* 188.18), be influenced in her pronunciation of 'mememormee' by the name of perhaps the most popular, after the 'Ave Maria', of prayers to Mary, the 'Memorare'.

But above all other considerations I see in this word the reflection I have been searching for of the Dantean vision. I suppose I may be conditioned in part by Hopkins's handling of trinitarian expression in his 'As kingfishers catch fire . . .', but then Joyce may have been, too (see my *Pauline Vision*, pp. 94–6).

Hopkins in the sestet of this sonnet plays with the pun on 'I' and 'eye' in theological ways that, I judge, would have intrigued, perhaps delighted, Joyce the lover of words.

> I say more: the just man justices;
>   Keeps grace: that keeps all his goings graces;
> Acts in God's eye what in God's eye he is –
>   Christ. For Christ plays in ten thousand places,
> Lovely in limbs, and lovely in eyes not his
>   To the Father through the features of men's faces.

'Just' is a term that Hopkins uses in its full biblical and theological sense of union with God, and 'grace' is the sharing in the inner life of the Trinity. Now follow 'eye', 'eye' and 'eyes', expressive of the all-seeing Trinity, and punning on the three 'I's of the three Persons. The 'I' of the Father and the 'I' of the Son are singular, but the 'I' of the Holy Spirit multiplies as the Word-made-flesh, the full gift of the Holy Spirit, shines out through the eyes of every loving human face.

This 'kiss of the mouth' of the Canticle of Canticles (a phrase loved by Hopkins as by Joyce) I see in 'Bussoftlhee', which seems to include the phrases 'But softly' and 'Buss soft hee' (*FW* 628.14). Lips to take that kiss could bring the keys like Boucicault's Arrah-na-pogue of *FW* 385.22 (Arrah, like Molly with the seedcake, passes the keys to her imprisoned brother as she kisses him), and perhaps (with the help of the masquerading Sh(a)un and Shem) achieve that Egyptian 'passing of the key of Twotongue Common, with Nush, the carrier of the word, and with Mesh, the cutter of the reed, in one of the farback, pitchblack centuries when who made the world' (*FW* 385.3–7). Maybe Anna receives the keys from the kiss of the Father and the Sons.

But how apt to express the kiss of the Holy Spirit, the full sharing of the three divine infinite personalities, is Anna's 'mememormee'! It seems to express Anna's realization that, on a literal level, as a creature of memory, understanding and will, she reflects the divine Trinity, and, on a symbolic level, as the Holy Spirit, she is, even more than the other Persons, the God of creation. Here in Anna's word it becomes possible to feel the full impact of the Dantean vision, though with the emphasis shifted, as in Hopkins's sonnet, to the Holy Spirit rather than, as in Dante, having it focused on the Word. The Miltonic double 'e' assures the emphatic stress on the last syllable. The 'me, me' of 'one of the littlest' (*FW* 170.14–15) and the 'me' of the 'chippy young cuppinjars' (*FW* 621.15–16) may indicate the direction toward birth Anna is taking, as well as the wild motion toward death which the 'meself' of *FW* 627.27 seems to involve.

'Thousendsthee' (*FW* 628.14–15) easily suggests to me the trinitarian dynamic activity. In 'Pied Beauty' Hopkins attempts to express the truth that the young Stephen rather badly missed in his use of 'an esthetic stasis' in his effort to build a Thomist esthetic (*P* 106). 'Static' implies a pause in motion, a destruction of motion. Stephen should have used a term for transcending motion – 'ecstasy', perhaps. I suppose Stephen is thinking in musical terms, of a Brahmsian long hold of a discord to dissolve finally into satisfying chords or trails of sound. But *that*, though it beautifies rhythm, is not the rhythm of beauty. To achieve beauty involves an experience, not at all interfering with motion, which by some unmoving but by no means static power transcends motion. Hopkins in 'Pied Beauty' treats of dualistic norms of beauty, the Brunonian contrasts by which we recognize created beauty, and in his final 'he fathers-forth whose beauty is past change: / Praise him' he does what limited, lying human language can do to point to the infinite dynamism of the Trinity. God does not interfere with or negate motions; He *is* past it. The still center of the turning wheel is another and less adequate effort to express what transcends expression.

'Thou sends thee' can be taken as a similar effort to express the totally mysterious divine processions. It can be apprehended in an orthodox Augustinian context, though it also can be read as an echo of Stephen's mocking Sabellian creed – 'and Himself sent himself' (*U* 197) – but it need not be. I interpret it, at any rate, as a human effort to express the intense personal love and activity of the Trinity – that which the term 'circumincession' was coined to express – though of course Anna could be using it in some personal context with no awareness of any theological possibilities.

Anna has rejoiced in 'the keys to dreamland' derived from her union with her husband (*FW* 615.28), and in a more theological context, how he promised to 'give me the keys of me heart' (*FW* 626.30–1). The heart is the symbol of the Spirit (*FW* 486), and it is trinitarian agreement that opens the heart to union – 'seeming-such four three two agreement cause heart to be might' (*FW* 612.24–5). Anna's words, as they strike my ear, suggest an analogy with Dante's ecstatic openhearted union with the infinite Trinity.

With that background I find the five nouns (or adverbs, or adjectives, or mixtures) which follow to suggest Anna's survey of what led to this union which is both ending and beginning. A *way* to be ('Be! Verb umprincipiant through the trancitive spaces! . . . A way', *FW* 594.2–5). She has come, like all human beings, basically alone, feeling last yet feeling loved too (maybe). It's been a long road. Each word is introduced by an 'a', the sign of indefinite being, really of dependent, accidental being, of abstraction. It is an article proper to the Druid's world, the world in the head, in the imagination, a world limited by human powers. 'A' deals with dreams as in Prospero's 'We are such stuff as dreams are made on', ephemeral, unreal. 'A' is 'Diu!' (*FW* 598.9). Duration, a mere passing of time, no lasting existence, no basis for a real present – that is 'a'. While 'diu' operates, 'the' has no chance ('The has goning at gone, the is coming to come' *FW* 598.9–10). The present is an illusion, it would seem, and 'the' as a designation of a definite being, an existing limited creature, is, like Stephen's 'I.I', merely a passing pointer in a Heraclitean flux. But another context for 'the' is suggested in Hopkins's great Heraclitean sonnet, the 'Resurrection', that lifts the temporal into union with the eternal. And in *FW* 'Adya' (598.14), Sanskrit for 'today', suggests, like 'Shantih' at the end of *The Waste Land*, that 'diu' will come to an end when the eternal sun rises. McHugh's *Annotations*, p. 598, supplies the apt comment from *Isis Unveiled*, celebrating 'the emanation of the objective from the concealed'.

Anna realizes that she must pass – 'The way I too. . . . What will be is. Is is' (*FW* 620.28, 32). 'Is', the name of God, expresses the timeless being of God as 'will be' and 'was' do not. From a divine theological stance, only 'is' can deal with the divine, which alone endures – 'is' alone 'is', as Anna says, thus neatly providing Egyptian divinity for herself, 'Isis'. In trinitarian theology, neither 'a' nor 'the' has any proper place, since articles point to distinct created entities, abstract or concrete, unlimited or limited. But if you have finally opened your heart with a *yes* or an *is* – the youthful Hopkins wrote in his notes on Parmenides: 'But indeed I have often felt when I have been in this mood and felt the depth of an instress or how fast the inscape holds a thing that nothing is so pregnant and straightforward to the truth as simple *yes* and *is*'[20] – then a Druidic 'a' will no longer do. 'The' can carry you to the real, either by hooking on to a real independently existing being like 'riverrun' and carrying through the cycles of creation or – it may be – by disappearing into the inexpressible glory of infinite being, into the ecstatic eternal breathing forth of the Spirit of Love – 'l'amor che move il sole e l'altre stelle'.

Notes

1   *James Joyce, A Portrait of the Artist as a Young Man*, ed. Chester G. Anderson (New York, Viking Press, 1968), p. 215.

2   New York, Viking Press, 1939.

3   William T. Noon, SJ, *Joyce and Aquinas* (New Haven, Conn., Yale University Press, 1957).

4   St Augustine established the basis for the rainbow imagery: see 'On the Creed', trans. Rev. C. L. Cornish, *Nicene and Post-Nicene Fathers*, ed. Philip Schaff (Grand Rapids, Mich., Wm B. Eerdmans Publishing Co., 1956), vol. III, p. 371. This is the trinitarian doctrine behind Stephen's discussion of fatherhood in 'Scylla and Charybdis': 'Fatherhood, in the sense of conscious begetting, is unknown to man. It is a mystical estate, an apostolic succession, from only begetter to only begotten. On that mystery . . . the church is founded' (*U* 207).

5   Noon, op. cit., ch. 6, pp. 105–25.

6   Patrick V. Rizzo, in *The Explicator* (Fall 1979), offers a defense of Berkeley: 'Berkeley's philosophy denies an external, independent veil hiding reality.'

7   *The Artist as Critic: Critical Writings of Oscar Wilde*, ed. Richard Ellmann (New York, Vintage Books, 1968), p. 369.

8   See my *James Joyce's Pauline Vision: A Catholic Exposition* (Carbondale, Ill., Southern Illinois University Press, 1978), p. 5. I quote the German version

of 'Lo, how a rose ere blooming' – 'Es ist ein Ros entsprungen . . . von Jesse kam die Art.'

9 A splendid article on the Trinity in the *New Catholic Encyclopedia*, by Robert Leo Richard, SJ, clearly sets forth the history and content of Catholic doctrine.

10 I have a chapter analyzing that lovely poem in *Metaphor in Hopkins* (Chapel Hill, NC, University of North Carolina Press, 1961), ch. 3, 'The Shekinah', pp. 45–70.

11 *A Portrait of the Artist as a Young Man*, ed. J. S. Atherton (London, Heinemann Educational Books, 1964), p. 250.

12 I use throughout the meticulous translation of Charles S. Singleton, translator and commentator in *The Divine Comedy*, Bollingen Series LXXX (Princeton, NJ, Princeton University Press, 1970), hereafter referred to as Dante.

13 *Portrait* (Heinemann edition), p. 250.

14 Dante, *Paradiso*, 2; commentary, p. 438.

15 Dante, *Paradiso*, 2; commentary, p. 584.

16 I discuss those with application to *Ulysses* in the *New Catholic Encyclopedia* under 'Allegory', and with application to 'Grace' in *The James Joyce Quarterly*, 'Swiftian Allegory and Dantean Parody in Joyce's "Grace"', vol. 7, no. 1 (Fall 1969), pp. 11–21.

17 Roland McHugh, *Annotations to Finnegans Wake* (Baltimore, Johns Hopkins University Press, 1980), p. 618: '8 & 20 to 5 = 4.32'.

18 In Willard Potts (ed.), *Portraits of the Artist in Exile: Recollections of James Joyce by Europeans* (Seattle and London, University of Washington Press, 1979), p. 223.

19 Adaline Glasheen, *A Wake Digest* (Sydney, Sydney University Press, 1968), pp. 73–4.

20 *The Journals and Papers of Gerard Manley Hopkins*, ed. Humphry House (London, Oxford University Press, 1959), p. 127.

James Joyce
and
his readers

Afterword: reading *Finnegans Wake*

CLIVE HART

For forty years and more most of us have been frightened of *Finnegans Wake*. Unsure how to respond to it, but hoping to establish some firm ground beneath our feet, we have concentrated overwhelmingly on detailed *explication de texte*, to the exclusion of critical commentary which would say something about the impact of the whole. Although large and usually deferential statements about the universality of its themes have appeared from time to time, not many critics have managed to guide us towards a satisfying aesthetic perspective. It is not even clear that most of us try to read it as we read other books. Do we believe that *Finnegans Wake* offers us that *frisson*, that sense of delighted participation in creative imaginative achievements with which we are familiar from reading 'The longe love, that in my thought doeth harbar', or *Twelfth Night*, or *Ulysses*?

Perhaps it can do so, and it seems important to try to find an answer. So far, however, we appear to be in some doubt. The difficulties are many, including not only the book's notorious density of reference and multiplicity of linguistic signs, but also its confusingly, disturbingly mixed tone. We hear many voices without knowing which, if any, to believe. Are we invited to participate directly in 'And low stole o'er the stillness the heartbeats of sleep' (*FW* 403.5)? Are we being addressed with ironic impatience in 'Shake it up, do, do! That's a good old son of a ditch! I promise I'll make it worth your while. And I don't mean maybe' (*FW* 209.14–16)? It does not help that the latter tone tends to predominate: a semi-exclamatory, slightly dismissive prickliness which both invites participation and simultaneously holds us a little apart.

The mixed tone may also be at least partly responsible for a disparity, which I know I am not alone in registering, between image and reality, between my sense of the book in tranquil recollection and my immediate impression whenever I have it open before me. Trying to maintain an uneasy grip on the whole, I inadvertently simplify it when remembering it. *Finnegans Wake* is richer, denser, than anything I can carry in my head. The same was true to a limited degree even of Joyce who, as the manuscript evidence shows, frequently forgot about some of the embellishments he had intended to include. (By contrast I tend to remember some other books, e.g. *Howards End*, as richer than they prove to be on rereading.)

It is perhaps inevitable that the gap appears to grow with increasing knowledge: the more one understands of the detail, thanks to the continuing flow of explication, the more difficult it becomes to sustain a satisfying sense of the whole. With some qualifications I nevertheless think it is worth our while to undertake the three centuries of meticulous work to which Joyce said he had condemned the professors. Some decades ago the task of explication was often undertaken in the expectation that patient research would lead to the elucidation of a mystery, on the analogy of the deciphering of Linear B. Despite the increasing production of specialist lexicons and annotations, much less is heard these days of comprehensive 'dictionaries' of *Finnegans Wake*. Not only our longer experience of the book, but also the growing familiarity of ideas of uncertainty, probability, approximation and open systems of thought, has led us to understand and to accept that in so far as there is a 'mystery' in *Finnegans Wake* it is fundamental, and fundamentally insoluble. Acceptance of 'mystery' at local level is, however, less easy. Ordinary human curiosity and frustration at bafflement combine to motivate the pursuit of meaning. When confronted by a strange word we naturally want to know what it means and why it takes this form rather than another. Virtually everything in *Finnegans Wake* was shaped with teasing forethought; almost nothing was left to chance. Distortions of ordinary English are not introduced because they are vaguely suggestive. Biographical and manuscript evidence, and the text itself, establish beyond doubt the dominance of semantic units, rationally controlled.

Many local delights arise from the pursuit of information elucidating the strange forms. At a microcosmic level it enriches one's sense of harmony and proportion to know that 'osghirs' (*FW* 241.32), which in the first place refers to Oscar Wilde, also contains the Armenian word for 'gold'. Placed in a context of scorn at worthless, destructive betrayers, the passage reads:

> They whiteliveried ragsups, two Whales of the Sea of Deceit, they bloodiblabstard shooters, three Dromedaries of the Sands of Calumdonia. As is note worthies to shock his hind! Ur greeft to them! Such askors and their ruperts they are putting in for more osghirs is alse false liarnels. The frockenhalted victims!
>
> (*FW* 241.28–33)

There is much here that I do not understand. Among other things, however, an antithesis is established between the golden worth of betrayed, calumniated Oscar, and the accursed, blabbing accusers who are not worth a red cent ('liard'). A taste for such perceptions of detail is easy to develop. After a good deal of preparatory research, *Finnegans Wake* is an excellent *livre de chevet*. The interrelationships of image and idea within a short paragraph, reread and pondered with a general if imperfect sense of the whole book in the background, frequently afford the same kind of aesthetic delight which one experiences in reading a short and highly wrought lyric such as Yeats's 'Leda and the Swan' (whose essential materials and double vision are of a kind that Joyce found congenial). A minor example is offered by Question 10 of I. vi: 'What bitter's love but yurning, what' sour lovemutch but a bref burning till shee that drawes dothe smoake retourne?' (*FW* 143.29–30). Here Joyce rewrites Philip Rosseter's song: 'What then is love but mourning, / What desire, but a self-burning, / Till she that hates doth love return?' It grows both more bitter and more ironic: 'What makes love (more) bitter than the experience of yearning, what sours our lovematch as much as the brevity of our burning which lasts only until the (sophisticated) fairy-like, cigarette-smoking beloved herself returns to smoke?' An additional, and very Joycean, element is introduced with the spelling 'bref': the burning in the spirit and in the loins is ironically and antithetically reflected in the burning of a

(Scandinavian) letter. The plaintive letter which echoes through-out *Finnegans Wake* is here transformed into a lover's *billet doux*, only to be cynically destroyed.

Local delights, even when they poignantly express recurrent themes of central human significance, are hardly a sufficient justification for struggling with a book of over 600 pages. Although reading *Finnegans Wake* in breaths of more than a paragraph or two can be unusually arduous, we are still in need of a satisfactory perspective which will allow us to respond more fully to the whole. While the outlines must inevitably remain less sharply defined than those of *Ulysses*, which Joyce thought he might have 'over-systematised', we need a better, a more satisfying sense of the movement, the rhythm, the shape of *Finnegans Wake*. Unless we are to wait another two and a half centuries, that sense will inevitably be based on incomplete evidence about the nature of the constituent parts. For various reasons I believe that this may matter a good deal less than in the case of books conceived in more conventional modes. In perhaps exaggerated form, Joyce suggested as much in a comment to Heinrich Straumann, Professor of English in Zürich: 'One should not pay any particular attention to the allusions to place-names, historical events, literary happenings and personalities, but let the linguistic phenomenon affect one as such.'[1] We should be guarded in the weight we give to this. Joyce notoriously tempered his remarks to the tastes and background of his listeners; a Dubliner would almost certainly have been given different advice. It none the less seems clear that Joyce did not necessarily expect all the constituent details to be elucidated before the book could be read. It is an approach which I think worth cultivating at the present time.

I do not yet know how to read *Finnegans Wake*, but the more I can learn to read it simply, the happier I believe I shall be. Now that we have learned to understand a good proportion of the detail – and above all now that we have a reasonable grasp of the kind of materials from which it is built – I am inclined to advocate quite rapid reading. Unless one is willing to ignore local difficulties and to make the best of rather cursory attention to complexities, a grasp of the whole is, in my experience, very nearly impossible. For such a reading I suggest adopting the working hypothesis that, with the exception of three main kinds of phrase and a few

other unclassifiable words, most of the text has a basic English
sense, or sometimes two parallel senses, as in everyday punning.
This basic thread of English sense we should always try to hear as
clearly as possible, since it usually supplies the primary meaning
of the book. The three main exceptions are (1) phrases specifically
written in a foreign language and often signalled by italics (e.g.
'*Hircus Civis Eblanensis!*', *FW* 215.27); (2) proper names and
initials; (3) some exclamatory words and phrases which lie, so to
speak, outside the controlling syntax of the text (e.g. 'Hou! Hou!',
FW 11.35). Allowing 'the linguistic phenomenon [to] affect one as
such', one absorbs additional meanings *en passant*, but with the
emphasis always on a consecutive reading. Two examples may
help to make the point, one simple, the second more difficult to
accommodate to my proposed method:

> Liverpoor? Sot a bit of it! His braynes coolt parritch, his pelt
> nassy, his heart's adrone, his bluidstreams acrawl, his puff but
> a piff, his extremeties extremely so: Fengless, Pawmbroke,
> Chilblaimend and Baldowl. Humph is in his doge. Words
> weigh no no more to him than raindrips to Rethfernhim. Which
> we all like. Rain. When we sleep. Drops. But wait until our
> sleeping. Drain. Sdops.   (*FW* 74.13–19)

In offering the following simplified version I do not wish to
reduce this marvellously evocative passage to a flat paraphrase,
but to propose that we attend to an underlying English utterance
which holds the paragraph together:

> Is his liver poor? Not a bit of it! His brains are like cold
> porridge, his pelt is nasty, his heart's droning, his bloodstream
> is crawling, his puff is but a 'piff', his extremities are *in*
> *extremis*: he is fangless, broken, has chilblains and is as bald as
> an owl. Humphrey is in his dotage. Words weigh now no more
> to him than do raindrops to Rathfarnham. Which we all like:
> rain when we sleep. Drops. But wait until our sleeping train
> stops.

Much of what is omitted from such a version is obvious: the
animals in 'His braynes coolt parritch' (the donkey's bray, the
pigeon's coo, the young salmon in parr-), not to mention
Humphrey's itches; the role-call of Dublin place-names; the drain
in which all ends; above all, of course, the play of vowel and

consonant. Most significant for my present purposes is the priority I give to 'nasty', in 'his pelt's nassy', over the more directly relevant 'damp' (German *nass*): his skin is clammy. For a moderately practised reader of *Finnegans Wake* 'damp' is the primary sense here. I nevertheless advocate trying to hear 'nasty' first.

For my more difficult example I return to the passage involving Oscar Wilde, quoted above (p. 157). I cannot 'hear' it all in English, but suggest the following as a beginning:

> Those white-livered ragsups (?): two whales from the sea of deceit; those bloody, blasted shooters, three dromedaries from the sands of Calumdonia. As are not worthy to shake his hand. Our (?) grief to them. Such askers and their Ruperts (?), they are putting in for more 'oscar', and are all false Lionels (?). The fainthearted victims!

('Oscar' is a slang word for money.) Apart from the lexicon, a difficulty, encountered quite frequently in *Finnegans Wake*, is presented by the syntax of the sentence beginning 'Such askors'. It is broken-backed, and one must do the best one can.

I do not suggest that the whole book will respond satisfactorily to this technique. Some passages mix so much non-English material into the English syntax as to make a simple paraphrase unworkable, as for example in the first sentence of the following:

> Dayagreening gains in schlimninging. A summerwint spring-falls, abated. Hail, regn of durknass, snowly receassing, thund lightening thund. (FW 607.24–6)

'Day-greening' may perhaps make some sense. Joyce, writing about the dawn, produces a semi-calque on Swedish *daggryning* (dawn) which, however, literally means 'day-greying' rather than 'day-greening'. But 'gains in schlimninging'? The phrase, evidently including German *schlimm* (evil), yields no English echo to my ear.

Joyce composed *Finnegans Wake* using a technique akin to that of the creator of a mosaic. He selected appropriate particles of material to build up a large picture, sometimes finding the bits and pieces ready made, sometimes making them himself and storing them in notebooks ready for eventual use. Not only have we concentrated too often on the exact shape and structure of the bits, but we have hesitated to accept Joyce's assurance to Straumann that the whole is sufficiently visible even if our focus on the detail is often blurred. In proposing the pursuit of a thread of English meaning I believe that some points of obscure detail will be unexpectedly clarified and that we shall develop a better sense of the proportions of microcosm to macrocosm. It is all too easy to be 'lost in the bush' and cry in desperation: 'It is a puling sample jungle of woods' (*FW* 112.3, 4).

I plead for a simple reading for two further, related reasons. First, it is clear that a vast amount of redundancy is fundamental to the structure of *Finnegans Wake*. Not only does Joyce tell the same archetypal stories over and over again, but a given phrase will often say the same thing in two, three, or even more ways. That 'bludgeony . . . Sunday' (*FW* 176.19–20) is a Bloody Sunday, because of the bludgeons; the erector of myths is also master of them, Mister Rector ('myther rector', *FW* 126.10). Even when the meanings contradict rather than complement each other, as here, missing much of the sense often leaves us less badly off than we might suppose. At first it is frustrating to find that clarification of a local difficulty, after much hard work, merely leads to a statement parallel to one on a neighbouring line. Later, however, one takes comfort from the knowledge that remaining difficulties are unlikely to be obscuring a solution to the mystery of the universe.

I also seek a simple reading because I should like to pay as much attention as possible to the surface. We need, I believe, to see *Finnegans Wake* more clearly, rather than to read through it. Its exploration of structures and relationships, its colour, wit and pathos, achieved through immediacy of image and pattern, offer an inexhaustible commentary on how to look at the world. If we read it for abstract ideas it serves us ill. *Finnegans Wake* does not seem to me to be a book of profound philosophical significance. The playing with time and space in 'The Mookse and the Gripes', the confrontation of unity and diversity in the Buckley–St-Kevin pages, are inventive, amusing and emotionally charged, but say nothing of consequence about philosophy. Again, much has been made of Joyce's interest in scholasticism and the Middle Ages, of which I believe he knew and understood very little. Nor does *Finnegans Wake* seem to me to have anything illuminating to say about linguistic theory or literary history: the famous quarrel with Wyndham Lewis strikes me as in itself an argument of low intellectual calibre which rapidly grows boring. We are misguided, I believe, if we read *Finnegans Wake* in search of Joyce's views on his literary contemporaries, on Irish politics, or on the controversies involving the Catholic Church.

I hope *Finnegans Wake* is more than the compendium of remarks about modern life, the super-commonplace book which many explicatory articles make it appear. I hope, too, that it is more than some recent nervous and self-protective modernist critics would have us believe. It is possible that Joyce wrote more than 600 pages over a period of more than sixteen years merely to explore the 'question of putting expressly and systematically the problem of the status of a discourse which borrows from a heritage the resources necessary for the deconstruction of that heritage itself',[2] but, if so, *Finnegans Wake* is reduced to a massively redundant and tedious exercise in denying the powers of the creative imagination, a 'literary exemplar', as Margot Norris puts it, of 'destructive discourses of the twentieth century'.[3] I hope, in fact, that *Finnegans Wake* is more than a pathological expression of the fear of authority, and that clear-sighted scrutiny of its surfaces through repeated rapid readings such as I have been advocating will show more of its freely imaginative constructive power.

In so far as post-Joycean writing may be invoked to place *Finnegans Wake* in context, I find it more profitable to appeal to the practitioners than to the theoreticians. And it is more useful, I believe, to try to read it in the light of *Marienbad*, of Pinget's *L'Inquisitoire* and *Quelqu'un*, than by comparison with more radically deconstructive work such as one often finds in the pages of *Minuit*. In *Quelqu'un*, as in *Finnegans Wake*, the sword of certainty never falls. Strenuous attempts are made in both to reconstruct simple narrative truths, but the pieces won't fit. In neither case do we lack information – indeed, we have a superfluity of it. I should like to be able to read *Finnegans Wake* as I read *Quelqu'un*: responding to a bustling and varied surface filled with evocative, lively and amusing detail, and listening to the wide-ranging registers of human speech. The banalities which make up the detailed utterances of *Quelqu'un* never tempt us to believe that anything profound is being said: it is a delightful interplay of images and minor events, the constructive juxtapositions being much more interesting than the self-evident point that the book also pulls to pieces the traditional structure of narrative reminiscence. And at the end one is aware that, against the odds, a shapely whole has emerged, expressing something which approximates to the total content of a small world.

I should also like to appeal to *Marienbad* and *L'Inquisitoire*, the scope and aspirations of which more nearly approach those of *Finnegans Wake*. Although neither Robbe-Grillet nor Pinget would thank me for saying so, their châteaux suggest, if not the universe, at least whole complex worlds of experience. In exploring both we learn to accept that ultimate truths about those worlds are not merely difficult of access but non-existent. In experiencing both we need to exercise our eyes and ears as much as possible, and our abstracting faculties as little as possible. Again, like *Finnegans Wake* both use as a basic dynamism an interplay of fixed points and fluidity. In all three works the contradictions, the shifting perspectives, the changing emphases are made a great deal more disconcerting by the presence of some elements which are either wholly or almost wholly stable. Aggressors and victims are sometimes confused, the same event occurs in summer or in winter, the shape and furnishing of a room change inexplicably. But as these surrounding circumstances modulate, the personalities of central, plaintive consciousnesses remain identifiable, while the structural relationships, sometimes painful, remain as inescapable determinants of the universe.

Finnegans Wake is itself an afterword. After the Word of the beginning we are left to explore a fallen, post-created world in which things do not always hang together. Although fallen it is not quite wholly chaotic. Nor does it lack beauty, harmony and local wholeness. Less transcendental than some would have him, Joyce savoured the 'audible-visible-gnosible-edible world' (*FW* 88.6). Like *L'Inquisitoire*, *Finnegans Wake* explores the multifarious nature of existence by reflecting it, by offering itself as a simulacrum. If they were to give the reader the sense of participating in something on that scale, both books had to be long, quasi-inexhaustible, and beyond the reach of total recall. No rejector of physical reality, Joyce celebrated it, reproduced it, represented it for our delighted apprehension. As in *Ulysses*, as in the novels of Pinget's middle period, the world of *Finnegans Wake* is essentially one of urban human interaction. The best things in it are the most immediately human: the Shem chapter (*FW* 169–95), the portrait of Issy (*FW* 143–8), Shaun's self-revelation and HCE's monologue in Book III seem to me to show *Finnegans Wake* at its most successful. I believe we may have heard too much about Joyce the revolutionary, the ironist making rude gestures towards the fiction of the past. While he wanted to 'make it new', the emphasis was on the making, on the creation of something to enhance our sense of life. Freed, like his successors the *nouveaux romanciers*, from the old constraints of 'character', Joyce nevertheless created highly individual human consciousnesses. The more directly we can perceive their relations with each other and with the curious environments in which Joyce placed them, the less tempted we shall be to treat *Finnegans Wake* in dreary terms of socio-literary history and the more we shall be able to profit from its acute perceptions of the everyday world around us.

Notes

1 Heinrich Straumann, 'Last Meeting with Joyce', trans. Eugène and Maria Jolas, in *A James Joyce Yearbook*, ed. Maria Jolas (Paris, Transition Press, 1949), p. 114.
2 Jacques Derrida, 'Structure, Sign, and Play in the Discourses of the Human Sciences', in Richard Macksey and Eugenio Donato (eds), *The Languages of Criticism and the Sciences of Man: The Structuralist Controversy* (Baltimore, Johns Hopkins University Press, 1970), p. 252, cited in Margot Norris, *The Decentered Universe of 'Finnegans Wake': A Structuralist Analysis* (Baltimore, Johns Hopkins University Press, 1977), p. 122.
3 Norris, op. cit., p. 122.